Tennessee County History Series

TENNESSEE COUNTY HISTORY SERIES

"Wilson County"

by Frank Burns

Robert E. Corlew
Editor

MEMPHIS STATE UNIVERSITY PRESS
Memphis, Tennessee

Maps prepared by Reaves & Sweeney, Inc., Memphis, Tennessee

Manufactured in the United States of America

Designed by Gary G. Gore

ISBN: 0-87870-190-7

DEDICATION

To Dixon Merritt: Nestor
To Bill Frame: Mentor
To Hugh Walker: Pathfinder

Prologue

There have been in the development of Wilson County three well-defined periods of surge, growth, stability, pause, and collapse that are, curiously, only slightly related to national or regional cycles. Each period covered from forty to sixty years for its cyclical course. Between each there was a time of pause, inactivity, doldrums.

The First Age began with the selection of a county seat in 1802. From then until 1830 population growth in Wilson County was unimaginably rapid: 3,261 in 1800, to 11,952 in 1810, to 18,730 in 1820, to 25,472 in 1830. Thousands of families uprooted themselves and moved into the new land. The expansion was to create towns, such as Lebanon, Statesville, and Commerce, but it was largely a time of village development and cottage industry. There was a paper mill on the Cumberland River, landing facilities at Hunter's Point, a wool carding factory on Franklin Road, warehouse facilities along the river, and in 1828 a large factory to manufacture ducking cloth. However, mostly the economy rested on land, its produce, and the marketing facilities for such produce. Village formation was in the traditional pattern of Europe: a stream, a road or a crossroads with a church, a store, a school, a smithy, a mill—for grain or for lumber and sometimes both kinds. One Wilson County village was different.

Cainsville was platted and developed by George Cain in a fashion followed fifty or a hundred years later by subdividers.

The hard times that followed the War of 1812 were severe, but it was the Panic of 1837, coming as it did immediately after the administration of Andrew Jackson with all of the implications that the ending of that era of glory had, that put a period to the First Age. Published records document the pause. The Census of 1840 shows a decrease in population to 24,460. The Goodspeed history states that the businesses of the 1830s were, with only a few exceptions, also the leading businesses during the forties. And another source quotes a nineteenth-century manuscript of personal recollections, "In the spring of 1824 Brevard College, one of the leading schools of the day, was established. The school continued for about twelve years." Thus the closing of Brevard College coincides with the year of the panic. Moreover, genealogists have noticed, although they are not particularly concerned with the reasons why, that there was a substantial out-migration from Wilson County at this time. West Tennessee, then in its own expansion period, Dickson County, Lawrence County, North Mississippi, Arkansas, and certainly Texas, at this very time in a violent struggle for independence, attracted thousands of persons who had resided in Wilson County between 1802 and 1830. Family names prominent in county records of that time disappear from the local scene completely.

But the Second Age was already in birth. By 1842 Lebanon and Wilson County were once more enjoying good times, along with most of the nation. Farming flourished. An Agricultural Convention, held in Lebanon in 1839, asked the General Assembly to form a state Board of Agriculture. The silk culture craze hit the state in 1841. Boosters of silk manufacturing reached a peak of enthusiasm in 1842 when Governor "Lean Jimmy" Jones was presented a silk suit produced in Tennessee of material from Tennessee silkworms eating Tennessee mulberry leaves. LaGuardo was one center of this industry. The era of agricultural fairs also began at this time. The first biennial state fair was held in Nashville in 1855 and in 1858 the Wilson County Fair was first held. A divisional fair was held in Lebanon for the first time in

The southwest corner of the Public Square in Lebanon in 1859 contained retail stores on the ground floor, professional offices above, and a covered walkway in front, each store boasting a hitching post of stone. Above the roofs of the store buildings may be seen the chimneys and roof of the Odd Fellows Hall that faced West Main Street.

1853 and William Goldston won the harness race at the 1856 divisional fair. This is important principally because the brother of Goldston's daughter-in-law was to become the famous harness race driver, Ed "Pop" Geers, whose home on the Nashville Pike has been marked by the Tennessee Historical Commission.

But the real life blood of prosperity was carried along the new roads built by the private turnpike companies under Whig-sponsored legislation. One of these roads was the magnificent Hermitage Turnpike, now U.S. Highway 70. Lebanon became the center of an elaborate system of post roads that covered the Southeast. The legendary Colonel M. A. Price was the magnate of mail contractors. In 1850 he owned 12,000 miles of mail routes under such government contracts. His stables were filled with fine horses, bred in Wilson County for coach horse quality. Manufacturing boomed. The Tennessee Manufacturing Company was established in 1844 with a payroll of 500 persons. By 1846 it had 2,000 spindles and 21 carding machines and was producing a thousand yards of cloth a day. In 1854 W. W. Carter established the Lebanon Flour Milling Company, the largest mill in Tennessee, shipping flour directly to Liverpool for the English market. In 1854 William Grisham erected a three-story textile manufacturing plant in northern Lebanon. In the same area were a hemp factory and the Harlin & Glass rifle factory.

The event that transformed Lebanon and shaped the town's character during the middle of the century was the establishment of Cumberland University in 1842. The event, sponsored by Robert Looney Caruthers and other men made wealthy by boom times, marks the birth of the Second Age. By February 1844 a magnificent new college building, planned by the noted architect William Strickland, stood on South College Street. By 1859 the law school was the largest in the nation and already its graduates were on the benches of state supreme courts, in the halls of Congress, and in the administrative chairs of a dozen other colleges.

The Civil War was a shock that almost finished the South, but Wilson County's Second Age did not end. Postwar society was changed very little from that of antebellum decades. Cumberland was still the center of cultural life, law students continued to come from all over the nation to Lebanon, and those who had led the community from 1842 to 1861 continued to be leaders, with the conspicuous exception of some who had supported the Lincoln government. Of these, only William Bowen Campbell and William Grannis were forgiven, the former doing much to ameliorate the course of Reconstruction in the county. By the middle 1870s agriculture, based mostly on farms of less than 100 acres occupied by their owners, placed Wilson first in the state in production of wheat, sorghum, butter, and horses; second or third in cedar lumber for export, grass seed, hay, barley, clover, hogs, sheep, and mules. The railroad fever that marked Reconstruction brought a short line, the Tennessee & Pacific, to Leb-

On the first Monday of each month the mule was king in Lebanon. The street livestock market was held on the Public Square until 1939, when the state highway department insisted that it be moved. For another 15 years Lebanon was the premier mule market of the state and in the 1980s the livestock sales continue to be large.

anon to 1869. The following year the county shipped out over this line in dollar value ten times the amount of forest products exported the year before.

On the night of December 13, 1881, the two-story brick courthouse building on the southeast corner of the Public Square burned. It was a symbolic event. Built in 1848, at the peak of the Second Age when prosperity was at a high point, it was destroyed when the economy of the entire South was beginning to suffer. In 1873 cholera had left death and disaster in its wake in Wilson County. Main lines of railroads had passed by to the south and the north, leaving Wilson and the counties of the Upper Cumberland isolated. Cumberland University was struggling, hat in hand, to operate on nickels and dimes. There had been significant deaths. Leaders of the old order—Nathan Green, Sr., Robert L. Caruthers, Robert Emmett Thompson, Edward I. Golladay,

William B. Campbell—passed on. For a decade or more Lebanon and Wilson County lived in a hiatus.

The first light before the dawn of a new day was the opening of Lebanon College for Young Ladies in 1886; the second was the first trip into Watertown of a train of the Nashville & Knoxville Railroad on December 12, 1889. Next was the laying of the cornerstone of Memorial Hall of Cumberland University in 1892. Full daylight came in 1902—Castle Heights School was opened; the saloons, which had been a retrogressive force in the business and commercial picture for three decades, were closed by law; and the Tennessee Central Railroad came to Lebanon—all in 1901–1902.

For reasons of their own, the Louisville & Nashville Railroad and the Nashville, Chattanooga & St. Louis Railway, together with the steamboat companies operating on the Cumberland River into Kentucky, had never wanted a through rail line between Nashville and Knoxville. It was in someone's interest to restrict access to the timber and coal wealth of the Cumberland Pleateau. Jere Baxter broke the power of the eastern financial interests, although he himself was eventually broken, and prosperity returned to Wilson County. It was a watershed. Those who had money ready to get in on the ground floor of the new period of expansion and vision are still spending their profits in the person of their children and grandchildren. Those who did not see the light in time or did not possess the resources went to their graves in genteel poverty. It was as simple and brutal as that. The Third Age rode into Lebanon on a TC locomotive. The Lebanon Woolen Mills opened in 1908. A young capitalist president of Cumberland University, David Earle Mitchell, who made his money in coal and timber, built a library, a chapel, a dormitory, and a heating plant for the college. Flour mills, hotels, theaters, electric lights, new brick buildings, residential mail service, a thriving wholesale trade, and automobiles rushed into Wilson County, bringing gold, silver, stocks, and bonds with them. In part it was due to a growing national economy, but one should remember what Dixon Merritt wrote in *The Lebanon Democrat* in 1934: "For some reason, Wilson County and Middle Tennessee are not feel-

The marble monument erected in Cedar Grove Cemetery in the family plot of Dr. David Earle Mitchell is the largest ever placed in Wilson County. Walter Smithwick *(sixth from left)* and Claude Seagraves *(on monument's right)* erected the stone, which was moved on a track of greased sleepers.

ing the full effect of the Great Depression. There is hardship, it is true, but not of the sort I have seen on the streets of New York. There are men out of work, but not as many as in Chicago or Cincinnati."

John Edgerton of Lebanon, president of the National Association of Manufacturers, was the voice of the Third Age before World War II. Afterward William Donnell Baird, president of the Tennessee Municipal League and chairman of the Tennessee Agricultural & Industrial Development Commission, was the voice of the industrial development of 1951–1965. By 1969 the Third Age was over, victim of its own growth. The great interstate highway that was so long anticipated helped to finish it. Lebanon was no longer the center of a trading area but was absorbed into the larger trading area of Metropolitan Nashville. The expansion of the metropolitan area outward along the superhighways that made commuting easy transformed West Wilson County into a bedroom with little sense of the bonds that tie community together. Exaggerated urban growth strained available services beyond the capacity of government to provide them. One particularly critical area was waste disposal systems. Pioneers did not worry about garbage disposal. Mid-twentieth century American families found it to be a major expense to the taxpayer and a source of controversy. It is ironic that the great Sesquicentennial celebration of 1969 which brought together every element of the community for one last gesture of solidarity was also unwittingly a wake.

By 1978 there were signs of the beginning of a Fourth Age. It is not within the scope of this narrative to read the future. Here at the gate that closed the 1960s, the 175th year after the first permanent settlement of Wilson County, the 150th after the granting of a municipal charter to the town of Lebanon, this story will pause.

$\mathcal{W}$ILSON County is located in the Central Basin of Tennessee and lies in the valley of the Cumberland River and its tributaries, Stone's River and Caney Fork. Early documents describe the county as "the land that lies along the south bank of the River Cumberland." From the beginning point at Drake's Lick in the northwest corner it is bounded by Davidson, Rutherford, Cannon, DeKalb, Smith, Trousdale, and Sumner counties. Its emblem is the cedar tree, more properly called the Virginia juniper, and its principal landmark is the Cedars of Lebanon state park and forest, the largest surviving forest of virgin red cedar in the world. Topographically its surface is rolling, except for high hills in the vicinity of Statesville, separated by hollows and the branches of several streams which flow into one of the three major rivers that surround Wilson County.

When the white man came there were no human inhabitants. It was hunting ground. The land was densely forested. The timber was large, tall, and thick. The big trees, with no underbrush around them, stood twenty to forty feet to the first limb. They made an almost unbroken canopy of shade. In many places cane grew much taller than a man. The forest was interrupted only by a few rocky glades here and there among the dense cedar brakes. The trees included oak, of the white, red, post, chinquapin, water, and other species; ash, both white and blue; scaly-

1

bark, pignut, and other hickories; black and sweet gum; white, red (or cork), and slippery elm; sugar, birdseye, swamp, and silver maple; black walnut; yellow poplar; chestnut; wild cherry; buckeye; red mulberry; beech; sycamore; cottonwood; hackberry; linn (linden); sassafras; box elder; dogwood; ironwood; red and black haw; hornbeam; holly; redbud; persimmon; branch willow. And there were the red cedars.

The low and level ground near the Big Spring, where the town of Lebanon was to rise, was a canebrake surrounded by a vast cedar forest. To the founders it suggested the Biblical name of the place of cedars. To the animals of the forest—buffalo and bear, panther and deer, otter, muskrat, and raccoon—and to the Indian hunters drawn to the spot by the plentiful game that the great, ever-willing spring refreshed, it was a rendezvous and a place to quench thirst. Much later one of the first settlers was to repeat the legend of that spring: "If you drank of its waters, in after years you would surely return to drink once more of its delicious waters."

The land was by terms of a royal charter part of Carolina. It was first explored by Europeans who left no written record yet discovered. The French came from Vincennes in the north to trade from a stockaded post on the bluffs at the French Lick, where Nashville now stands. The Spanish came from the south, the English from the east. There were earlier shadows in old lore: Vikings, Welsh, Phoenicians. In 1748 there was Dr. Thomas Walker and his party; in 1763 the Wallen party; in 1765 the Henry Scraggins (or Scaggs) party; and Colonel James Smith's party in 1766–1767. There were the five trappers and hunters from South Carolina led by Isaac Lindsey who came in 1768, meeting by chance Michael Stoner and James Harrod (or Herrod) on Stone's River (which by that time bore the name of one of Smith's group, Uriah Stone—Smith's name was on a fork of the Caney Fork). And in 1769 the Long Hunters came, a large party that included Stone and Kasper Mansker. The creeks on the land that was to become Wilson were named by these early Englishmen—English still, but beginning to think of themselves as what they would soon be called—Americans. The Cumberland River was named, as all the other Tennessee Cumberlands were, by Dr. Walker for William, Duke of Cumberland, savior of the House of Hanover from Bonnie Prince Charlie in the uprising of the Forty-Five. Flowing into the river were, clockwise from the present Wilson-Davidson County line on the south bank of the river, Drake's Lick, Spencer's, Cedar Lick, Barton's, Spring, Cedar (first called Spruce), and Jennings; then Round Lick, into which Jennings' Fork emptied. Smith's Fork flowed into the Caney Fork River. Feeding Stone's River were Fall, Pond Lick, Sinking, Hurricane (pronounced harrykin), Sugg's, and Stoner's creeks. These are within the 1982 boundaries. Before October 26, 1799, when the third General Assembly of the State of Tennessee passed *An Act Reducing the Limits of Sumner County and Creating Two New Counties,* the land was called "that part of Sumner County south of the River Cumberland" and in the autumn of 1799 heads of families had signed, perhaps while attending a militia muster day, a petition asking the General Assembly to establish for their convenience a new county. The boundaries established in that act included in addition to what is now Wilson County a portion of the present Smith County as far east as Caney Fork, portions of the present Trousdale County, portions of the present DeKalb and Cannon counties, and perhaps a part of the present Rutherford. An Act of 1801 which redrew the eastern line of Wilson County along approximately the present Smith-Wilson boundary also stated that the line would run to "the Indian boundary" but a few days later another Act extended the county to the southern boundary of the state, although title had not then been acquired from the Indians. In 1813 Rutherford County acquired territory from Wilson to establish the present line, and in 1836 and 1837 Cannon and DeKalb counties incorporated the territory that they now contain east and south of the present line. In addition, the Act of 1801 moved the northern boundary of the county from low water mark on the south bank of the Cumberland to the middle of the river.

The county is well watered for livestock and humans alike. Potable water is generally that which is known as "blue limestone" but sulphur, chalybeate, and other mineral waters supplied such

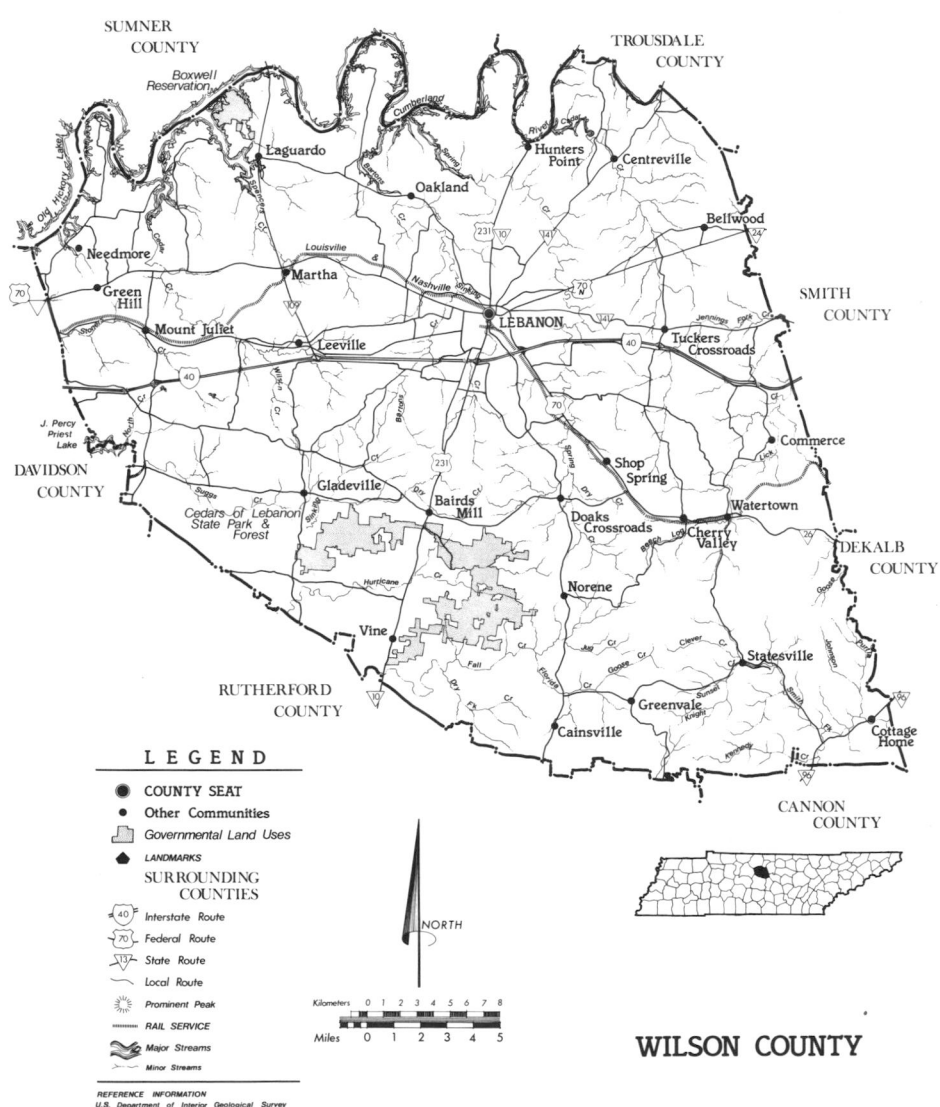

SUMNER
COUNTY

TROUSDALE
COUNTY

Boxwell
Reservation

Laguardo

Oakland

Hunters
Point

Centreville

Bellwood

Needmore

Louisville

Martha

Nashville

SMITH
COUNTY

Green
Hill

Mount Juliet

Leeville

LEBANON

Tuckers
Crossroads

J. Percy
Priest
Lake

Commerce

DAVIDSON
COUNTY

Gladeville

Bairds
Mill

Shop
Spring

Cedars of Lebanon
State Park &
Forest

Doaks
Crossroads

Watertown

Cherry
Valley

DEKALB
COUNTY

Hurricane

Norene

Vine

Statesville

RUTHERFORD
COUNTY

Greenvale

Cottage
Home

Cainsville

CANNON
COUNTY

L E G E N D

● COUNTY SEAT
• Other Communities
Governmental Land Uses
♠ LANDMARKS
SURROUNDING
COUNTIES

40 Interstate Route
70 Federal Route
13 State Route
Local Route
Prominent Peak
RAIL SERVICE
Major Streams
Minor Streams

NORTH

Kilometers 0 1 2 3 4 5 6 7 8

Miles 0 1 2 3 4 5

WILSON COUNTY

REFERENCE INFORMATION
U.S. Department of Interior Geological Survey
State of Tennessee Department of Transportation

resorts as the Fountain of Health, Hamilton Springs, and Horn Springs well into the twentieth century. Wells and natural springs are plentiful and small farm ponds, constructed with the aid of state and federal agencies after 1933, provide water for livestock, curb excess runoff, and are sometimes stocked with fish. The intensive development of suburban residential tracts has caused some surface water to be tainted with pollution.

In the neighborhood of Vesta are found the boomshaws, a geological oddity. They are cavernous pits of water in sandstone formations amid the all but universal limestone. They are not ordinary sinkholes caused by the erosion of subterranean streams nor the ordinary collapsed cave formations. One is 150 feet across and is locally reputed to be "bottomless" although it is known to drain beneath the surface into a stream that is a tributary of Stone's River. The name is of Indian, or possibly French origin.

The county is based almost wholly upon limestone, occurring in successive layers nearly horizontal in position. These belong to the group of formations called by geologists Lower Silurian, the upper 500 feet in the Nashville formation and the lower in the Lebanon formation. The hills and ridges in southeastern Wilson County are capped with flint and black shale. Lebanon is surrounded by a circle of moderate hills, the county seat itself being in the center of a depression or basin through which Town Branch of Barton's Creek flows and frequently overflows.

Before the urbanization of recent years, Wilson was one of the most productive agricultural counties of Tennessee. Except for cedar glades and some exposed rocky land, almost all of the soil could be cultivated.

Its Climate

It is said that only June and October make life worth living in Middle Tennessee. Then, if ever, come perfect days. Tennessee's greenness does come from the normally plentiful rainfall. Wilson County has a fairly temperate climate, but with wide extremes between occasional very hot, dry summers and very cold winters with moderate to heavy snowfall. The coldest recorded temperature was 22 degrees below zero in 1886; the hottest was

In August 1939 a freshet came down Town Creek and submerged the Public Square of Lebanon under four feet of water.

111 degrees in 1930. The deepest snowfall of record was 38 inches in 1886. The dryest year was 1980, with an 11-inch deficiency; the wettest was 1979, with an excess of more than 13 inches.

Those Who Came Before

One day in the 1930s a tenant farmer who lived on the Rome Pike came into the office of *The Lebanon Democrat* with something heavy wrapped in a newspaper. He set his package down on the desk of Hugh Walker, the associate editor, and opened it. Inside were two stone images, a male and a female. The larger, named on the spot "Rogo" by Walker, after its finder, Jeff Rogers, was called in an article in *Time Magazine* "the finest example of pre-

Columbian sculpture ever found on the North American con-
tinent." A full-page color photograph, made while the image was
on display at the Museum of Modern Art in New York City, accompanied the article. Rogo, later named "Sandy" by the Tennessee Archeological Society which placed his effigy on its emblem,
and his mate came not from the farm where Jeff Rogers was
living when he brought his package but from the Sellars farm
on the Sparta Pike, where he had previously lived as a tenant.
This is the location of the prehistoric Indian village whose great
central ceremonial mound was excavated in 1877 by a Harvard
University team headed by F. W. Putnam, curator of the Peabody
Museum. The village stood in the loop of Spring Creek to the
east of the community of Greenwood and it was one of the 11
enclosures with interior mound noted on the W. E. Myer map,
made for the U.S. Bureau of Ethnology. Also on that map are a
mound and cemetery on Smith Fork southeast of Statesville and
a burial cave at Statesville, a cemetery south of Cherry Valley,
and a double mound on the western slope of Egypt Hill about
six and a half miles south of Lebanon. The historian John Haywood records that in 1823 on a farm on Fall Creek there was
found a 15-inch female stone image, its head and face similar to
some that had been found in Mexico. Its present whereabouts
are not known. At other times and at other sites there have been
found pipes, pottery, a ceremonial birdstone, and in 1966 a ceremonial stone axe-scepter of excellent workmanship.

The Settlements

The first permanent settlement in Wilson County was made
in the autumn of 1794 after the Ore expedition to Nickajack and
Running Water effectively ended the menace of hostile Indian
attacks on the Cumberland frontier. The settlement was made
on the north end of Hickory Ridge, west of the present city of
Lebanon, near a bold spring at the head of Spencer's Creek by
John B. Walker, John Harpole, and others. Although permanent, this was an isolated location, and extensive settlement did
not begin until the autumn of 1797. There had been an earlier

settlement in 1790 on Stoner's Creek by John Cloyd and John Williamson. The house that Cloyd built still stands, a part of the house of his great-grandson Duncan Ligon, beside Highway 70 at Green Hill. On March 8, 1790, a child, Elizabeth Williamson, was born to John and Margaret Cloyd Williamson. Soon afterward there was probably a settlement on Sugg's Creek, as families moved eastward from Davidson County, this land being close enough to the forts for quick shelter. There may have been tilled fields on the south bank of the Cumberland River before 1794. John Wynne, a Virginian who had moved to North Carolina, came to Hickory Ridge early: 1797 has been reliably stated as the date of his first coming. In the latter part of that year William McClain and his father-in-law John Foster settled at Drake's Lick. Foster and others soon moved to the waters of Spring Creek, near the present center of the county. This became known as the "Donnell Settlement," because a large number of persons of this name had come there from Alamance, North Carolina. Others there were John Doak, David McGathey, and Alexander Braden. Round Lick Creek, first called Thompson's, was also the site of an early settlement. David Young was settled in that area by September 28, 1797, when his son James was born. John and Benjamin Phillips migrated to Wilson County from Library, Pennsylvania, in 1797, but the deeds to their farm on the west fork of Round Lick Creek were dated 1801. On Smith's Fork the settlement that later became Statesville, located at the confluence of Rocky Branch and Knight Creek, probably began in 1797. A number of its first settlers came from Halifax County, Virginia, and Rowan County, North Carolina, with a few from Rockingham County, Virginia. Originally called Maryville in honor of Mrs. William Bumpass, wife of the tavern keeper, it was renamed Statesville for the North Carolina town when postal officials said there already was a Maryville, Tennessee. The first true community of the village type was Center Hill, located east of the present Doak's Cross Roads near Dry Fork of Spring Creek. Here stood the first building of Spring Creek Presbyterian Church, first church in the county, as well as the first school, established by Benjamin Alexander. There was a grist mill, and as early as 1802 a cotton gin established by George Alexander. In all probability Center Hill and the "Donnell Settlement" were the same. The likely date of settlement here is 1799, but families may have lived there as early as 1796.

Families may have lived within the present boundaries of Wilson County as early as 1780, or at least heads of families may have been on the land. The names of persons receiving land in the Cumberland settlement from the State of North Carolina because they were on the land before June 1, 1780, are recorded in a document in the National Archives in Washington, a communication from James Glasgow, Secretary of State of North Carolina, dated July 30, 1791. In addition, they are listed, with the acreage and location of their grants, in a volume in the North Carolina archives, reprinted in facsimile as *North Carolina Land Grants in Tennessee*. The legislative act was adopted in April 1782. The original act establishing a "military reservation" in Tennessee, providing western land for North Carolina soldiers of the Revolution, took effect June 1, 1780. The preemption rights given in the act of 1782 protected those who had gone onto the reservation lands and settled before that date. James Robertson himself, "The Father of Middle Tennessee," received such a grant. Locations which can be identified as within the present boundaries of Wilson County, and the grantees, are:

James Bradley, Thompson's Creek (now called Round Lick); Rowland Madison, Barton's Creek; Bartlett Searsey, Stoner's Creek; John Caffrey, south fork, Stoner's Creek; Thomas Davis, south side of Cumberland; Richard Simms, Sinking Creek; Peter Looney, south side of Cumberland; Thomas Jones, Cedar Creek, south side of Cumberland River; William Fletcher, Spring Creek; James Harris, headwaters of Stoner's Creek; Peter Looney, Sinking Creek; Christopher Beesley, Stoner's Lick Creek; Nicholas Conrad, Spring Creek, south side of Cumberland; Philip Conrad, Barton's Creek, south side of Cumberland; William Goosney, Barton's Creek, south side of Cumberland; George Kannady, west side of Cedar Creek; John Dunham, Spencer's Creek, south side of Cumberland; William Stewart, on Spring Creek; James Mulherrin, south side of Cumberland; William

McWhirter, on the fork of Sinking Creek; Perry Graves, south side of Cumberland; Ebenezer Mann, small branch below Sinking Creek; Anthony Bledsoe, south side Cumberland, three miles above Drake's Lick. These names and locations are listed as in Glasgow's certified list. Some of them are listed again in a legislative act of 1784 reaffirming the preemption grants. Some locations are ambiguous. There is a Barton's Creek in Montgomery County. Stoner's Creek flows west into Davidson before it empties into Stone's River. The south side of the Cumberland embraces a wide expanse. In this latter case every precaution has been taken to find supporting reasons to believe that that particular grant lay between Drake's Lick and the mouth of Round Lick Creek. (Those listed in the 1784 act are Bradley, the two Conrads—there called Conroe—, Fletcher, Goosney, Harris, Kannady, Looney, Madison, Mann, Simms, and Stewart.)

There is no assertion here that these settlers remained on the land. Exposed to Indian attacks in the crucial autumn of 1782, given a respite after the Treaty of June 1783 until the Cherokees violated the truce in the spring of 1784, under violent assault from 1785 to 1789 and again from 1792 to 1794, the early cabin builders abandoned their small clearings in a wilderness and retreated to the protection of the forts and blockhouses. There could be no permanent settlement of Wilson County until after the Ore expedition to Nickajack in 1794. But it is unlikely that persons who came to the Cumberland country in 1779 and 1780 would have settled in Davidson, Sumner, Robertson, Montgomery, Williamson, and Trousdale counties (using the present names and boundaries) while leaving this great fertile chunk of the Cumberland Valley between Stone's River and the Caney Fork empty, especially when more than a score of them had good title to the land. It is probable that the first settlers—or cabin builders—in what is now Wilson County came in the fall of 1779 and the spring of 1780, either with James Robertson or John Donelson or with the South Carolina group that included John and Alexander Buchanan, the Mulherrins, Daniel and Sampson Williams, and Thomas Thompson, and were here either continuously or intermittently until the summer or fall of 1784 when

Indian hostility forced them back to the protection of Fort Nash-borough. It is likely that they or their heirs returned and became permanent settlers, probably after the Ore expedition but per-haps not for another two or three years.

In the tax list of Sumner County for the year 1795 it can be determined from the names of creeks mentioned that Captain Richard King's company of militia comprised the part of Sumner south of Cumberland River. Those listed are Robert King, 640 acres between Spring Creek and Round Lick Creek; James Campbell, Ephrim Farr, John Hamilton, John Lowrence, Robert Patton, and James Vinson on Sinking Creek; David Wilson on Spencer Creek; Thos. White on Jennings Creek; Nathan Parker on Round Lick; John Grenaway on Barton's; Betsy Barrow, Mat-thew Barrow, and James Barrow on Round Lick; Hardy Murphy (Murfree?) on Barton's; Malacahy White on east fork of Spring; John Howell on Round Lick; Barnard Tatum on Cumberland River, Cedar Creek, and Spring Creek.

Although it is probable that the Hickory Ridge settlement was made in 1794, not until 1797 was full-fledged settlement, clearing, tilling, and village-making begun. In the Goodspeed history is the traditional and often quoted statement that the first settlement was made in the year 1797 at Drake's Lick, by William McClain and John Foster. This statement, and another that the first male white child born in the county was Josiah McClain, born at Drake's Lick on January 1, 1799, were exploited in nine-teenth century political campaigns by McClain, long the county court clerk. Historian Dixon Merritt asserted that the issue was a deciding factor in at least seven campaigns and finally ended at least one official career. But some weight must be given to the tradition because it first appears in print as a report of a personal interview with the mother. The 1797 date is supported by the lack of confirmation of births in the county before that of James Young in September 1797, except two recorded in the William-son and Cloyd family Bible. Furthermore, the Green Hill area was in and out of Davidson County until 1803, the actual county line being uncertain until even later. Although descendants of Perrigan and Sarah Nelson Taylor, early settlers on Cedar Creek, say that a daughter, Margaret Nelson Taylor, who married William Maxey in 1815, was born in Wilson County in 1796 and George Washington Smith, a veteran of the Battle of New Orleans and the War for Texas Independence, was said to have been born near Drake's Lick in 1795, these are unsupported by documentation.

The coming of the Seawell, Wynne, and Mabry families is never dated earlier than 1797; usually the date given in printed sources is 1799. Even in the James Vaulx Drake history, which dates the first permanent settlement as occurring in 1794, the date for construction of improvements such as mills, churches, and schools is 1796 or later. Drake records that Thomas Conyer's water mill on Barton's Creek three miles northwest of Lebanon was built in 1796 but adds "it is thought." The earliest transactions in deeds recorded in Book A, Register's Office of Wilson County, occurred in 1798. On December 11 of that year Henry Turney bought 640 acres on the headwaters of Barton's Creek from John Lankester (*sic*) and on December 14 Samuel Barton transferred all his property to his children. It is conceded that Barton and Lancaster had to have been in possession earlier but nothing shows them on this land before 1797. Standing against these arguments are the names on the 1795 tax list. However, although some of the surnames appear on the petition to establish the county, none of the full names do. These may have been, like David Wilson, nonresident landowners.

The Cabin by the Spring

Edward Jacobs was born in Ireland about 1769. He was shipwrecked off the coast of North Carolina in about 1779 and was rescued by Lumbee Indians, who reared him. In about 1785 he married an Indian girl, Layula. Their daughter, Sallie, was born in 1786. The following year when Neddy, as he was called by everyone, was eighteen years old, they left the Indians. After living in Carolina for a time, they joined a party of settlers bound for the Cumberland Country, probably in 1790 or 1791. It is likely that the family lived in Davidson County for some time before building the cabin that stood by the great spring where

The rear part of this log cabin was the home of Neddy Jacobs and his family, first settlers on the site of Lebanon. Located northwest of the Town Spring, it was first moved to the Dillard farm south of Lebanon in the 1830s. The front cabin was then added. Both were dismantled when Interstate 40 was built.

the town of Lebanon was to be built. All sources agree that the cabin was built in 1800.

Sallie Jacobs married John Dillard, lived to the age of 102, and died in 1888. She told her story to her great-granddaughter, Mrs. Rowena McIntyre Fowler. She said that she was a "good-sized girl" when the family came to Tennessee "though it had not then been named Tennessee" and had a clear memory not only of settling at the spring but of the journey over the mountains and across the wilderness. Encounters with Indians were frequent on the trip but no harm came to the party. Layula, who was said to be a "princess," had some emblem of her "royalty" (or perhaps priestesshood) and would put this on when showing herself to the Indians. They always recognized this and it constituted a badge of safe passage for the party.

The Jacobs cabin was simple, with a stick chimney and a dirt floor. It stood on what is now the southeast corner of West Market and North Maple streets, below the spring where its stream flowed into Town Creek. The land belonged to James Menees, a resident of Davidson County. When the family built its first house the country around was all either cedar forest or dense canebrake. There were bears to kill for meat and oil, turkeys to be lured from the cane with a "turkey caller," uncountable flights of wild pigeons, and animals drinking from the spring. There were also two deserted cabins nearby. The Jacobs house was not really the first. In 1802 the great spring caused the selection of forty surrounding acres as the location of the county seat. After this Jacobs built a new cabin with a puncheon floor. It is recorded that he would sit and fiddle by the hour, putting aside his beloved instrument only to go hunting or fishing to replenish the family larder. It is not recorded that he bothered to purchase his town lot when the auction was held on August 16, 1802, the named buyers being William Allen, William Bloodworth, William Crabtree, William Gray, S. Harpole, John Impson, John Irwin, Edward Mitchell, James Peacock, J. Providence, Peter Rule, M. Stewart, William Trigg, and John Wright. In 1803 Allen opened the first store and Mitchell the first inn. Impson built the first proper house, it too being by the spring.

When Sallie Jacobs married, Neddy killed a dog, tanned the hide, and made her a dressy pair of wedding slippers. It was not his only skill. His Indian foster parents had taught him to be a medicine man. When a cholera epidemic came (it must have been either the terrible first visitation of the disease to Lebanon in 1835 or the scourging of 1849), Neddy was an old man but doctors were few and the need was great. He practiced Indian medicine throughout the epidemic and cured many, all whom he could reach before the disease became too far advanced, with what is believed to have been an herbal concoction of dog fennel.

In the early 1840s, perhaps in 1841, the Jacobs cabin—the second floored one, for the first had been torn down by Neddy—was acquired by Nelson D. Hancock who was operating a saddle shop in Lebanon but who owned a farm on what is now called the Tater

Peeler Pike. He removed it to that farm, along with a second cabin, and the two, joined, stood there until construction of Interstate Highway 40 past the site caused their demolition in 1965.

Before Neddy's death some of Layula's Indian relatives or friends or fellow tribesmen came to see her. She went away with them and never returned. Where did she go? Tradition is silent. Was it at the time of the Cherokee Removal? Did she take the long and arduous pilgrimage to the new Indian nation in the West? Did she walk the Trail of Tears? Perhaps, for that trail did pass near if not through Lebanon in 1838, when Layula Jacobs was nearly 70.

Organization of the County

By midsummer of 1799 settlement of the land between Stone's River and Caney Fork, south of the Cumberland, had advanced to the point that a new county, to be taken from the southern portion of Sumner, was perceived as necessary. On July 25, 1799, a petition was drawn up, stating:

> To the General Assembly of the State of Tennessee:
> The petition of the Inhabitants of Sumner County living on the South side of the Cumberland River humbly sheweth that your petitioners have now a suficant number of Elective men to entitle them to a new county bounded on the North by Cumberland River from Davidson County up to the Confluence of the Cany fork then East to the Indian boundary which will leave a suficant bounds for the County of Sumner and a new County to the East of it which will leave the South side of said river in the situation that would be proper for a further division which will be necessary in a short time. Your petitioners further pray that if any such attempt should be made that your honorable body will not suffer the County of Sumner to cross Cumberland River and your petitioners as in duty bound shall ever pray.

The body of the petition appears to be in the handwriting of John Merritt, whose name is subscribed immediately beneath. Nearly 300 signatures (or marks) follow. Many of them, like John Merritt, had been supposed by their descendants to have arrived

in Middle Tennessee after 1799. Also, names of others thought
to have been pioneers do not appear. It is possible that the latter
did not sign because they were not asked or because they were
not in favor of establishing the new county. Two other petitions
were filed at almost the same time. These were signed by residents of the area north of Cumberland River eastward from Rocky
Creek (in present Trousdale County) and by "sundry the inhabitants of Capt. Harpole's militia company." The latter included
none who signed the July petition but many whose names appear on the earliest extant tax lists of Wilson County. The "Harpole" petition, submitted to the General Assembly on September
19, 1799, asked for the new county line to be drawn from the
mouth of Rocky Creek south southeast to the Indian boundary.
This would have placed all of the present county east of Lebanon
in another new county; as the "Merritt" petition had proposed
two counties the issue seems to have been over the location of
the dividing line. The petitions all state clearly the reasons for
partitioning Sumner:

> The great extent of said county and our local situation render
> it very inconvenient and disagreeable to attend courts, general
> musters, and many other public meetings that we are obliged to
> attend, as many of us live at least fifty or sixty miles from the place
> of holding courts. . . . It will be a means of quelling several parties
> and factions which almost distract said county and without which
> your petitioners as well as many others living on the extreme parts
> of said county will be left in a state of anarchy.

Wilson County was created October 26, 1799, by an act of the
Third General Assembly, Section 4:

> And Be It Enacted, that another new county be established by
> the name of Wilson, to be contained within the following described
> bounds: beginning upon the south bank of the river Cumberland
> at low water mark at the mouth of Drake's Lick Branch, the north-
> east corner of Davidson County, thence with the line of Davidson
> County to the Cherokee boundary as run and marked agreeably
> to the Treaty of Holston, and with said boundary to the Caney
> Fork and down the Caney Fork according to its meanders to the

mouth thereof, thence down the meanders of Cumberland River by the south bank to the beginning.

It was provided that a court of pleas and quarter sessions be held in the new county, to meet on the fourth Mondays of December, March, June, and September, and that the first court be held at the house of Captain John Harpole. On the day the Act was passed, Governor John Sevier appointed as Justices of the Peace for Wilson County John Alcorn, Charles Cavanaugh (more often spelled Kavanaugh), John Doake (correctly spelled Doak), Andrew Donelson, Elmore Douglass, Matthew Figures, William Gray, John Lancaster, William McLean (more usually spelled McClain), and Henry Ross. Some months later the governor commissioned as militia officers John Wynne, lieutenant colonel commandant; Edward Mitchell, first major; William Steele, second major; James Anderson, Elisha Dillard, Kanah Eikals (Elkanah Echols), Solomon Harpole, William Lancaster, captains; Theophilas Allen, Joseph Bishop, Charles Cavanaugh, John Eikals, Jacob Spickant, lieutenants; Jonas Bishop, Martin Harpole, Robert Smith, Samuel Steele, Hugh Telford, ensigns.

Local government being based on captain's companies until the Constitution of 1834, the appointments had geographical significance. Indeed, from the places of residence of the ten justices it is possible to determine that the boundaries of what would later be called civil districts were drawn perpendicularly south from Cumberland River: the first, or westernmost, Captain Elisha Dillard's company, represented on the court by William McClain (Drake's Lick) and Andrew Donelson (Green Hill); the second, lying along Spencer's Creek and Cedar Lick, Captain Elkanah Echols, represented by William Gray (Spencer's) and Henry Ross (west side of Hickory Ridge); the third, lying along Barton's Creek and its headwaters, Captain James Anderson, represented by John Alcorn (lower Barton's Creek north of present Lebanon) and Charles Kavanaugh (upper Barton's Creek east of Hickory Ridge); the fourth, along Spring Creek and Cedar (first called Spruce) Creek, Captain Solomon Harpole, represented by Matthew Figures (Cedar Creek) and John Doak (upper Spring Creek); the fifth, along Round

Lick Creek and Smith's Fork to the Caney Fork, Captain William Lancaster, represented by Elmore Douglass (lower Round Lick Creek near the present location of Rome) and John Lancaster, who had moved to the present village of Lancaster in 1798, selling his land along Barton's Creek, and building a mill, a shop, and a store at the confluence of Smith's Fork and Caney Fork.

The senior militia officers resided in the center of the more thickly populated district. Colonel Wynne lived on Hickory Ridge not far from Tucker's Gap. Major Mitchell lived opposite the "twenty-five mile tree" (which tradition locates at the junction of Stumpy Lane and Tater Peeler Pike a short distance south of the present Lebanon—25 airline miles from Nashville on Town Creek Branch of Barton's Creek). Major Steele lived on upper Cedar Lick Creek not far from the present Leeville.

On November 6, 1801, the General Assembly passed an act that detached from Wilson and added to Smith County (which had been established in 1799 by the same act that created Wilson) all the land between the Cumberland River and the Indian boundary from Caney Fork westward to the present county line. Thus the controversy reflected in the "Harpole" and "Merritt" petitions was compromised by dividing the eastern lands into two fairly equal portions. An act of November 13, 1801, appointed a commission to locate a site for the county seat. To this body were named Christopher Cooper, who lived on Sanders Fork in the far southeastern part of the county; Dr. Alanson Trigg of Fall Creek; Matthew Figures of Cedar Creek, a miller who lived near the present site of Centreville; John Harpole, in whose home the court first met; and John Doak, who lived near the present Doak's Cross Roads. Doak wanted the county seat and the courthouse to be placed near his home—there was a spring, and the old road to the Holston passed by. But Harpole had seen a much larger spring, known far and wide to animals of the forest and the Indians who had hunted them, the spring where he and John Carr and Peter Looney had paused during their pursuit of the warriors who had sacked Zigler's Station at Bledsoe's Lick in 1792. The commissioners went to the spot: a fine fountain of crystal water shaded by a grove of virgin red cedar to which led well-beaten tracks of hunters and beasts. Below the spring stood a simple log cabin, built the year before by Neddy Jacobs for his wife and child. "This is the place," said Cooper.

Forty acres were purchased from James Menees, who lived in Nashville. Four other cabins were built after the sale of town lots on August 16, 1802; the builders were Edmund Crutcher, John and Thomas Impson, and Edward Mitchell. James Anderson built a house and secured license from the court to operate an "ordinary" there. The next year William Allen opened the first store in the county seat and a simple courthouse was built of cedar logs covered with riven oak clapboards. There were two jury rooms but no offices. It stood at an unidentified spot on the west side of the Public Square and was in use until 1811 when a brick building was erected in the center of the Public Square by William Seawell, contractor. A painting of this courthouse, discovered in 1976, shows it as a two-story structure with a hipped roof and an octagonal cupola with a bell and topped by a gilded eagle. In 1848 the third courthouse, designed by William Strickland, was erected on Lot 8 on the south side of the Public Square. It was of brick with Corinthian columns and a cupola; it had two stories with the circuit courtroom upstairs and the county courtroom and offices downstairs. This building burned in 1881. It was replaced on the same site by a large brick structure erected by J. F. Bowers & Brothers of Nashville and occupied in 1884.

This was also a two-storied brick structure with stone cappings, a mansard roof, and a brick portico on the north side. This building was enlarged in 1936–1937 by the addition of an annex for the offices of the county judge, school superintendent, health department, and American Red Cross. It was remodeled in 1948. For most of its life two large courtrooms, one for the county court and the other for the circuit court, with clerk's offices between overlooking the Public Square, were on the second floor with high-ceilinged offices for county officials on the first. The remodeling moved the trial courts into the county courtroom and divided the circuit courtroom into an extra floor for offices. The original architects, Smith and Rome, had estimated the cost at $18,000 and the completion date as April 1, extended to June 1, 1884. The final cost was $17,700 and the completion date May 28.

In 1965 inexorable dilapidation, obsolescence, and the lack of parking space caused county voters to approve construction of a new courthouse, which was to be located for the first time off the Public Square. Planners hoped to encourage development of the business district eastward to higher, less often flooded ground. A tract between East Main Street and East Gay extended was acquired, bonds were sold, Morton-Carter architects employed, and R. E. Hunt Construction Company accepted as general contractor. The bid was $925,000; the final cost $1,200,000. The building, constructed in Art Moderne style of brick, concrete and glass blocks, steel, concrete, and glass panes, was planned for efficiency, comfort, convenience, and future growth.

The county was organized around captain's companies until 1834 when the system of civil districts was introduced. In Wilson County there have always been 25 civil districts; however, voting districts, with boundaries adjusted after each U.S. Census, are used as precincts in elections and to choose county commissioners. The reorganization of the former county quarterly court into a county commission with a reduced membership (25 instead of 53), constant reapportionment with ever-shifting voting district lines (the result of the *Baker* vs. *Carr* "one man, one vote" lawsuit and the Constitutional Convention of 1977), the flight of population from metropolitan Nashville, and urbanization have all combined to demolish old loyalties, the old patterns of community development and growth, and the adhesive power of commonly shared interests and beliefs. It is for the next generation to interpret the eventual effect.

Andrew Jackson, Storekeeper

It is sometimes forgotten that Andrew Jackson had many business and land interests in Wilson County, was a taxpayer of both the county and the town of Lebanon, and claimed as close friends many residents of Wilson. Some of these were Colonel John Knibb Wynne, Dr. Henry Shelby, Dr. James Frazer, Dr. Sam-

This photograph of the Wilson County quarterly court was made after the July meeting in 1954. Standing in front are County Judge Turner Evans and County Court Clerk C. O. Dodson. Grover Foutch *(back row, fifth from left)* was the youngest member of the 1918 court. Serving until 1969, he was the link that bound together a hundred years of history.

uel Hogg, John Allcorn, Foster Doak, some of his Donelson in-laws, and young Sam Houston. He practiced law in Lebanon, was a frequent guest in various homes, and made many horse trades in Wilson County.

Perhaps then it was natural that the General should select Lebanon as the site of one of his early ventures into business. Jackson had a store at Hunter's Hill. In the spring of 1805 he moved this enterprise to Clover Bottom. In fact, he established what would be called today a shopping center where the road crosses Stone's River. He had drawn trade to the Hunter's Hill store from a wide territory. Wilson countians whose names are found on the old account book of that establishment include Patton Anderson, James Foster, John Hays, William McClain, James McFarland, William Moore, and John Williamson. These account books are very important to the historian because they help to date significant events in Jackson's life. For instance, because the dates in the Clover Bottom book show when it opened it is possible to fix the date the Jacksons moved into their new home, The Hermitage. It is regrettable that the book for the store in Lebanon has never been found.

As a matter of fact, the store at Lebanon preceded that at Clover Bottom. It may also have preceded the Gallatin store. Jackson and his wife's nephew, John Hutchings, acquired a location for a store on the Public Square in Lebanon in 1804. Walter Durham, well-known Sumner County historian, says that the deed to town lot No. 5 in Gallatin, to Jackson and Hutchings, was proved at the December session of the Quarterly Court in 1804. A building was then constructed on the lot, and Hutchings conducted business there, but this could not have been earlier than the spring of 1805, close to the date the Clover Bottom complex, which included "a store, a tavern, stables, and booths for hucksters," opened.

The site of Lebanon had been chosen for the county seat in 1802. There was already a house there, occupied by Edward Mitchell, and a cabin, occupied by Neddy Jacobs. (The owner of the land, James Menees, lived in Nashville.) After the auction of town lots, John Impson, Thomas Impson, and Edward Crutcher very soon had houses on their lots and James Anderson, who built his house near the town spring, had taken out license for it as an "ordinary" or tavern. After William Allen opened what is considered the first store in Lebanon in 1803, probably in the spring or early summer, it is generally believed that the Jackson and Hutchings store was the second. It was opened in the summer or fall of 1804, after Jackson had untangled himself from a partnership with a Thomas Watson. The lot, bought for $40, was No. 8 on the south side of the Public Square. It was bought by the county quarterly court in 1847 for $800 and was the location of the courthouse for 120 years.

"Gone to Texas"

The dispossessed have always moved westward. From Devon and Ayrshire, Monmouth and Derry, and from all Europe they crossed the Atlantic. From Pennsylvania and Virginia and the

Carolinas they crossed the mountains. From the Holston, the Watauga, and the French Broad they came into Middle Tennessee. They were not all dispossessed. All did believe they could better their lot. They all had a dream.

The Quest For Elsewhere

There was a man named Cornelius Gregory MacPherson. He was a teacher and an editor of a newspaper in Lebanon, Tennessee, in the nineteenth century. That is beside the point; his vocations simply fix him to a given locality at a given time. The point is that C. G. MacPherson was not fixed.

He was born September 26, 1806, in Halifax County, North Carolina, like so many other Wilson countians of his time. He died in Louisville, Kentucky. In between birth and death, he attended school at Princeton, Kentucky, and taught there, taught and edited in Lebanon, Tennessee, married a girl from Russellville, Kentucky, and taught school in four different states. His wife's family had lived in Maryland, Virginia, and Kentucky. She died at Jackson, Tennessee. Mrs. MacPherson was no more of a fixed point then her husband.

In 1950 a resident of San Antonio, Texas, Mrs. Frank Foster, wrote to the postmaster of Lebanon seeking information concerning her grandparents.

> I am told [she wrote] that they lived on the old cobblestone highway between Lebanon and Nashville. Their names were Organ. A son, John Chartres Organ, was born there; also a daughter Charlotte Fanning Organ. The family were near friends of the Fannings who were at the head of a school for girls, and three of the older girls, Martha, Cornelia, and Elizabeth, finished there in 1857 or 1858. This family lived in a two-story rock house. It was used as Army headquarters during the Civil War. They came to Texas and settled Fannin County, Bonham being the settlement they pioneered. They had eight children and came from Pittsylvania County, Virginia. They arrived in Texas on July 4, 1859.

Although genealogical researchers would have some problems—one being the presence of several persons named John Chartres Organ in Wilson County census records—it seems likely that this family is descended from Enoch Organ, who married Sara Templeton in Pittsylvania County in 1790, or from Neil (Cornelius?) Organ, who was 60 years old in 1830 and might have had a granddaughter, Cornelia, who finished her schooling in 1857 or 1858. Also to be considered is Rolley (perhaps originally Raleigh) Organ, who commanded the Horn Company, a mounted drill unit that paraded before Henry Clay in the 1840 presidential election campaign.

The point of the MacPherson story and of the Fanning-Organ story is that mobility and migration are not twentieth century innovations in America. Americans are and always have been a moving people and the movement has been along defined routes. From the late 1700s to 1900 many lines of migration from East to West funneled through Middle Tennessee. There were various reasons for this, some geographical, some political, a few ethnic. The movement was generally from Pennsylvania down the Shenandoah Valley into East Tennessee and from there down into Georgia, Alabama, and Mississippi or across the Cumberland Plateau to Middle and West Tennessee, Arkansas, and Texas. There were also other routes that brought up-country families from South Carolina, Quakers from Maryland and the Carolinas, many others from many places to Wilson County and from Wilson they went West. Josiah Chandler, for example, was born in England in 1762 and his wife, Sally Eddins, in Scotland in the same year. Married in England in 1784 they came to Charleston, South Carolina, the next year and stayed in that state for 15 years. A son, Andrew Chandler, was born there in 1789. The family moved to Wilson County in 1800 and built a two-story log house (until the 1970s it stood just off the Coles Ferry Pike in Lebanon). Josiah Chandler died there in 1827. In 1849, the year after his mother died, Andrew moved westward. It was a well-traveled trail.

Many of the first wave of emigrants from Wilson County went to Lincoln County, Tennessee, which organized its government in 1810. The first chairman of its county court was Philip Koonce who had been among the earliest settlers on Spencer's Creek near the present Leeville. It is thought that Elijah Alcorn, who entered land in Lincoln County in 1810, was a brother of John Alcorn, first Wilson county register, first postmaster of Lebanon, and county court clerk for more than 25 years. Elijah's significance is that he exemplifies another pattern of migration. He is believed to have removed from South Carolina to Georgia to Wilson County around 1800, then to have emigrated to southern Middle Tennessee before moving on to join the Austin Colony in Texas near Washington-on-the-Brazos. Elijah was one of the first emigrants to cross the Brazos River on December 31, 1822.

Sam Houston In Lebanon

Lebanon has never forgotten Samuel Houston. The site of his first law office, on East Main Street, is marked by a bronze plaque. And it is of record that Samuel Houston never forgot Lebanon.

The law office building, a small structure made of cedar logs, weatherboarded, stood until 1932. It was then owned by Rufus Doak, insurance man. The ball where Houston met Eliza Allen, his beautiful young bride-to-be, in 1828 was held in a house (Brittain Drake's) that stood west of Lebanon. Houston was governor of Tennessee at that time and in the summer and fall of that year he worked hard for the election of Andrew Jackson to the presidency. He and Jackson were invited to attend a ball at the Drake home, which stood near the present Martha Road. Eliza Allen was a sister of United States Representative Robert Allen. When Houston was in Congress he had been presented to Allen's teen-aged sister, a schoolgirl with violet eyes and braided blonde hair. Eliza was also a kinswoman of Robert L. Caruthers of Lebanon, and came to the ball at the Drake house in the company of some of her Caruthers kin. Houston saw her and was smitten by the 19-year-old beauty as he had not been by the schoolgirl.

The Allens recognized it as a promising match. Houston was not only governor, assured of reelection, a protege of the man who was sure to be president. Houston was also handsome, ambitious, and likely to be himself an aspirant to the presidency some day. He visited John Allen in Gallatin, as he had done before, but this time as a suitor. His suit was accepted. The marriage, celebrated at the candlelit Allen home on January 22, 1829, did not last, and history was made in its breach. Less than three months later they parted for reasons still known only to themselves but with repercussions that sent Houston to Texas in despair. There he met his destiny. He did indeed become President, but of the Republic of Texas rather than the United States.

There is a small oil painting of the Houston law office, done in the early 1930s by the Lebanon artist Annie Evertson. The simplicity of the little building is typical of the simple origins of many of America's great men. It is true that Washington, Adams, Madison, and Jefferson were men of wealth but Jackson and Houston were, like Lincoln, of frontier origin and fought their way to the top.

Henry Bruce's *Life of General Houston, 1793–1863* (Cambridge, 1891) testifies to the lasting place that Lebanon held in the great Texan's memory. Here he placed his foot on the first rung of the ladder of preferment. Before Lebanon, Houston was one of many. Afterward, he was marked for greatness. Bruce tells the story of Frederick Golladay, a young man of Lebanon who was traveling in Texas in 1853. When he arrived in Huntsville, where General Houston was residing, he became ill and sent word to the General that "a Golladay of Tennessee is lying sick" in his town. Houston came to the bedside, his first words being, "If you are the son of Isaac Golladay, I recognize you as the child of an early and true friend." He said that he knew Frederick's older brothers but had left Lebanon before the young man was born. He recalled in detail his early struggles as a young lawyer in Lebanon and how Isaac Golladay, his landlord and the postmaster, extended him credit for clothing and postage and recommended him to the good people of the town. Houston then came for him in his carriage early the next morning and took him to his own house where young Golladay was ill with a fever for ten days or two weeks. Frederick recalled that while a patient there Houston stayed up one whole night giving him medicine and bathing his feet in warm water. During this time Houston was in a reminiscent mood and described the scene of his taking leave of his friends in Lebanon for a wider field, making an emotional address to them in the Public Square.

Houston had come to the county seat of Wilson in December 1818 from six months of study with Judge James Trimble, who was astonished that his student was ready to pass the bar examination in so much less than the usual 18 months. Golladay felt confidence in the young man, furnished him a splendid wardrobe, stood good for his postage (25 cents a letter then), rented him the small building on the north side of "the East street" for a dollar a month, and then lent him the dollar. Houston set up his few legal books, hung out his shingle, and went to the courthouse to take the oath of an attorney. In 1963, Perry Johnson, circuit court clerk, found the entry in an old minute book.

Soon Houston was appointed adjutant general of the state with the rank of colonel and in October 1819 he was elected attorney general of the Davidson district, which made it desirable that he move his residence to Nashville. In the ten months in Lebanon Houston had traveled the road to Nashville many times; as The Hermitage stood not far off that road he stopped whenever possible at his old commander's home for amiable conversation which surely included the political plans of both ambitious men. In 1824 Jackson made an unsuccessful bid for the presidency. In 1827 Houston was elected governor. The next year saw Jackson, with Houston by his side, again a candidate.

On Monday night, June 12, 1978, a dinner was given on the campus of Cumberland College as the keynote event of the campaign of U.S. Representative Albert Gore, Jr., for reelection. There had never been such an array of public persons in Lebanon as gathered rather informally under the trees and around the Memorial Plaza in front of the main college building. The principal remarks to the crowd of nearly 1500 citizens of the Fourth Congressional District were made by Thomas P. "Tip" O'Neill, Speaker of the House of Representatives, the highest ranking incumbent public official to appear in Lebanon since Jackson's time. It was indeed a great occasion, but a hundred and fifty years before, almost to the day, there had been an equally great occasion in which Andrew Jackson and Samuel Houston played the central roles. An eyewitness account, written by Colonel Obadiah G. Finley, a veteran of the War of 1812 (whose son Jesse became a Confederate brigadier general), has been preserved. Finley wrote:

> I thought in this letter I would let politics alone; but must not omit telling you that Genl. Jackson and Gov. Houston just spent the last American anniversary [July 4, 1828] with us. We gave them a dinner at Mr. [Albert] Wynne's tavern [on the east corner of South Cumberland Street and the Public Square] that has not been equaled in the state for its extensive splendor. The Gen'l says he never saw one equal to it except one in the City of New York and one in New Orleans Jan. 8th last. In the evening we gave them a splendid Ball at Mr. Hallums.
>
> They were received 7 miles below town by a committee; two miles from town by the military—under a heavy fire and salute and marched to town by the military company and citizens to the extent of at least 3 thousand at least, where he was introduced and addressed until dinner, which was in Mr. Wynne's back yard, under a spacious awning. The table had four wings and contained 250 plates. You may judge of its extent. (At which I must say, though modestly and for your own ears only) They appointed me president of the occasion. I was assisted by your old friends, John Hall and Joseph Johnson as Vice Presidents. We passed the whole affair in good style—and escorted him to the Smith county line and gave them over to the authorities of Smith Co. who gave him a dinner in Carthage the day after.

"Lean Jimmy" Jones, Master of the Stump

In 1839 Newton Cannon, a Whig, was governor of Tennessee and a candidate for reelection. His Democratic opponent was James Knox Polk. The two met in a series of joint discussions. The speaking in Lebanon took place in a cedar grove on the east side of the present Cedar Street between East Market and Sycamore. Governor Cannon was a plain farmer from Williamson County before his election and although well informed on public issues he was a dull speaker on the platform. Colonel Polk, as he was then, had been a member of the Congress for several terms and was Speaker of the House of Representatives when he decided to enter the race for governor. In debate he was marked by shrewdness and tact.

The voters knew that Polk had resigned his seat in the Congress under the influence of former President Andrew Jackson so that in the crucial national election of 1840 Tennessee would be secured for the Democrats. In 1836, when Jackson had endorsed Martin Van Buren, the electoral vote of Tennessee had gone to Judge Hugh L. White of Knoxville, with Wilson County casting 1610 votes for White and only 553 for Old Hickory's choice. Jackson looked on Wilson as a second home, for many friends and comrades of the Battle of New Orleans were residents of the county and Jackson had owned much land, practiced law, and even kept store there. It is difficult to explain the Whig dominance of the county. Jackson and Houston were both popular there and leading families such as the Doaks and Andersons remained staunch Democrats. But for 20 years Wilson did not deviate from the Whig party except in legislative races. Perhaps Jackson's effort to anoint Van Buren as his heir, perhaps growing manufacturing and mercantile interests with natural affinity for Whig policies, perhaps strong local leadership by William Polk McClain, Jordan Stokes, and others turned the tide. At any rate in 1844 the son of the same Colonel Finley who proudly chaired the dinner for General Jackson in 1828 was riding a horse at the head of a parade for Henry Clay.

An immense crowd gathered to hear Polk and Cannon speak. Polk knew very well how to make use of laughable anecdotes. Cannon was more matter-of-fact. He preferred sound logic that was not very interesting. Moreover, a local favorite, John Bell, was present as a candidate for reelection to Congress from the Hermitage District (Davidson and Wilson counties). Before Cannon and Polk had closed their debate, the crowd had become very restless, so great was its eagerness to hear Bell, the idol of the Whig Party of Tennessee. Like Polk, Bell had been Speaker of the U.S. House of Representatives and both enjoyed a national reputation. It was late in the evening when Bell was presented to the large audience. One who was there recalled: "The

The house built in 1828 by Robert L. Caruthers stands on West Main Street. From its balcony Judge Caruthers is said to have delivered a speech accepting nomination for the governorship in 1863. Although he was elected, he was unable to serve because of the Federal occupation of most of the state. The builder was Joseph Reiff, who also built the Hermitage; the stairways are similar.

excitement was intense, the applause was deafening when he waved his hand for silence. And such a speech! The Democratic aspirant for governor was blistered 'cap-à-pie' [head to foot] but nevertheless he was elected. Tennessee was still wonderfully under the influence of the Battle of New Orleans."

Polk won the governorship from Cannon, although in Wilson County Cannon received 2273 votes to 1157 for Polk. Two years later Governor Polk was to meet his match on the platform.

At the age of 20, a tall, thin young man from Nashville had brought his 17-year-old bride to Lebanon, and the young couple moved into their new home on a farm a few miles north of town. That was in 1829. The young man was James Chamberlain Jones, one of America's great campaign orators. He was very slender and rather ungainly, six feet, two inches tall with a mere 125 pounds distributed over his frame, and so was nicknamed "Lean

Jimmy." He was born at a place called The Fountain of Health on the Wilson side of the Davidson County line in 1809. His formal education was limited but he read extensively in the library of his guardian, Col. Edward Ward. Eight years after he came to Lebanon he was elected to the state legislature and in 1839 he was reelected. In 1840 he was an elector on the Harrison and Tyler ticket. The next year, although he was only 32 years old, the Whigs chose Lean Jimmy as the candidate to beat Governor Polk, "The Plumed Knight of Democracy, the Invincible Orator," in his race for reelection.

Will T. Hale, in the history *Tennessee and Tennesseans* (New York, 1913), asserts that the art of "stump speaking" was originated in this campaign. The first of the Jones-Polk debates occurred at Big Spring in Wilson County on March 30, 1841. Jones was a natural mimic and actor, with great facility in turning a point against an adversary. Polk lost his temper. Jones kept perfectly cool, and, while looking as serious as a judge on the bench, told more jokes. The people laughed—but they got the point of Jones' anecdotes and elected him after a series of joint discussions throughout the state. The "stump speeches" of Polk and Jones had set a pattern for American campaign oratory for years to come. Again in 1843 the two were opponents and again Lean Jimmy defeated the man who was to become the next president of the United States. Not until 1861 was a Democrat able to carry Wilson County in a gubernatorial campaign. In 1845 Jones, the first native Tennessean to be governor of the state, left office and returned to his farm home. He became United States senator in 1852, left the Whig party to campaign for James Buchanan in 1856, was succeeded in the Senate in 1857 by Andrew Johnson, and died in Memphis in 1859.

Jones is the only Wilson County resident to serve as governor, although four others who at times made their homes here held the governorship. Sam Houston resided in Lebanon in 1817–1818 and began the practice of law at that time; William Bowen Campbell resided at Carthage while governor and moved to Lebanon at the end of his term in 1853; Robert Looney Caruthers (whose mansion, built in 1828, still stands on West Main Street

The largest political crowd of the twentieth century in Wilson County heard Governor Frank Clement open his campaign for reelection in 1954. The governor had been a resident of Lebanon and attended high school and college there.

in Lebanon), elected Confederate governor in 1863, could not take office because of Federal occupation of the state capital; and Frank Goad Clement resided in Lebanon while his father, Robert S. Clement, was attending law school and returned later as a college student himself. Likewise, Jones was the only native-born Wilson countian to serve in the U.S. Senate from Tennessee, although John Martin, born in Wilson County, was elected a Senator from Kansas in 1892. Senator Albert Gore was reared on Route 1, Watertown, on Round Lick Creek just across the Smith County line and attended Watertown High School and Cumberland Preparatory School. Jesse Wharton, appointed to the Senate in 1814, did build a fine home on Spring Creek near Lebanon in 1811 but, although the 900-acre farm was passed on to a son and Wharton descendants remained prominent in Wilson County affairs, he is generally described as being from Davidson County. Congressmen from Wilson County have been Samuel Hogg (1817–1819); Robert L. Caruthers (1841–1843); Robert Hatton (1859–1861); William Bowen Campbell (1837–1843, 1866–1867); Edward I. Golladay (1871–1873); and Haywood Y. Riddle (1875–1879). Caruthers was also a member of the Confederate Congress.

The "Lean Jimmy" Jones house, now occupied by the Rev. and Mrs. Hall Grime, was marked by the Tennessee Historical Commission. Much has been added to the original brick structure, the entire front portion and one wing of the Grime residence having been built after the Jones occupancy. The original house is at the rear and its distinctive brickwork can easily be detected. The Hunter's Point Pike formerly ran to the west of the structure and its front was then at the west. Before Jones bought the house it was owned by John Alcorn, first postmaster of Lebanon and county court clerk from 1802 to 1827.

Cumberland University

A college was established at Lebanon, Tennessee, in July 1842. It was both new and old. There is no doubt at all that it was an attempt by the General Assembly of the Cumberland Presbyterian Church to remove Cumberland College from Princeton, Kentucky, where it was struggling for lack of money, to a new location. This was Robert Donnell's intention, clearly expressed in open meeting, and he had been, in May 1842, made chairman of a committee of the General Assembly to receive bids for the location of a college. The committee met in Nashville on July 1 and accepted the bid submitted by the delegation from Lebanon: $10,000 in cash for the erection of a college building. The building was to be new, the location was new, the charter was new and the name, Cumberland University, in the charter was new. However, the president, Franceway Ranna Cossitt, and two of the most valuable members of the Princeton faculty, C. G. MacPherson and T. C. Anderson, did come to Lebanon from

President John Royal Harris *(front left)* and Dr. Winstead Paine Bone *(immediately behind)* lead the Cumberland University commencement procession of 1923 as it enters Caruthers Hall.

Kentucky; the relationship of the Lebanon school to the church was more or less the same as that of the Kentucky institution; and the constituency was the same. Moreover, the new charter was not issued until December 30, 1843, and the first Commencement program does call the school at Lebanon Cumberland College. (All this would have been moot if the union of the Presbyterian Church USA and the Cumberland Presbyterian Church in 1906 had not been only partially consummated and the sponsorship of Cumberland University made a matter of acrimonious litigation.)

But on a sunny September day in a little brick building on the street leading north from the Public Square, Professor MacPherson opened the first year of Cumberland in Lebanon. There were 45 students. The president, Dr. Cossitt, would not arrive until February, when the second term began. The college had no building of its own until two years later. But the 45 were to be the vanguard of a long line of children of this alma mater, thousands of them coming to Lebanon from all 50 states of the Union and from the five continents. Over a period of one hundred and forty years some 14,000 students have graduated from

Cumberland. They have occupied positions of trust throughout the land, as high as the United States Supreme Court, the premier office of the Cabinet, and the chairmanship of the most powerful committees of the Congress; they have been presidents of great schools, presiding officers of religious bodies, chairmen of great corporations and trade associations, have edited the newspapers and magazines and written the books read by the people, and have risen to positions of command in the armed services. Cumberland has proven itself truly a servant of the nation.

Within five years of that September day the university had started to train young lawyers, using a method of instruction that was almost entirely new to the profession and a textbook, Abram Caruthers' *The History of a Lawsuit*, that was itself to become a landmark of legal education. Within ten years the theological seminary would begin training young ministers, a school of engineering would produce civil engineers to survey the new western lands and build the roads to them, and a preparatory school was to train youth for admission to institutions of higher learning. Before 20 years had passed there were Cumberland graduates in the Congress, in the state capitols, on the trial and appellate bench, and in pulpits from New York to Oregon.

But the American Civil War slashed across the story of Cumberland like a saber stroke. From civil life the sons of the college went onto the battlefield, some to earn a general's stars, others only a shallow grave. When the war was over, the magnificent building on the shady campus on South College and West Spring streets was in ruins, burned during the last weeks of the war for no material reason. It was a symbol of the waste of war. On a fragment of a Corinthian column, after the cannon were quiet, a graduate of Cumberland, remembering Christopher Wren in the ruins of old St. Paul's, scrawled in charcoal, "Resurgam."

"I shall arise," W. E. Ward wrote, and arise Cumberland did, by sheer determination. The School of Law, which reopened around the Green family (whose members contributed to jurisprudence from 1831 when Nathan Green was named to the Supreme Court of Tennessee to 1947 when Grafton Green, Chief

Justice of that court, died) developed a hard-as-nails discipline of study which paid off for its graduates. Indeed, the real gift of the Cumberland University law school, looking back over its century and a quarter in Lebanon, was not so much its graduates who won fame and renown but rather the spirit of faith in the lasting tenets of democracy, passed on like an unfailing torch to five generations of young men and women. In 1871 the School of Law reduced its course of study from 15 months to two semesters. The one-year course, with concentrated study of textbooks, augmented by lectures and moot court practice, was adopted to meet the impoverished economic state of the South and Southwest after the Civil War. The intense study required to complete the prescribed work within the brief period allowed proved precisely the ingredient necessary to produce competent trial lawyers. The number of Cumberland graduates who attained success on the bench, in government, and in business is incredible. The Alumni Association determined and the publisher confirmed that by 1957 only Harvard University had had a higher percentage of its graduates listed in *Who's Who in America*.

Dedicated teachers remained at their posts for a lifetime. Nathan Green, Jr., taught the law for 63 years; Andrew Bennett Martin for 42; William Richard Chambers for 14; Albert Bramlett Neil for 13, sitting simultaneously part of that time as a judge of the circuit court; Samuel Burnham Gilreath for 30, a man whom the chairman of the legal education committee of the American Bar Association called "the finest teacher of law in America." Among other professors and practicing attorneys of shorter tenure with the school were Bernard Bailey, Edward Ewing Beard, Frank T. Fancher, Allison Humphreys, Jr., Charles Leaphart, Bromfield Ridley, Grissim Walker, Arthur Weeks, and Albert Williams.

In the hard days of Reconstruction the man who, more than any other, could be called the founder of Cumberland University once more came to the rescue. Robert L. Caruthers had been a member of Congress when the university opened its doors. He was elected the first president of the board of trustees and served as president until his death in 1882. In 1847 he personally guar-

Judge Nathan Green, Jr., is seated in front of his house on South Greenwood Street. A professor of law and chancellor of Cumberland University, he built the residence after the Civil War. Its garden, planned and tended by him, was famous throughout the state. The house burned more than 60 years ago and was replaced with the present dwelling in which his son, Chief Justice Grafton Green, lived until his death.

anteed the salary of the first professor of law. On October 1, 1847, the first recitation in the law school was held in his small brick law office in the side yard of his residence on West Main Street. In 1868, made feeble by the tribulations of war and the toll of age, he consented to become professor of law when the chair fell vacant and no younger man could be found to take it. He continued to teach, holding classes in the library of his residence, until near the time of his death. In 1877 he had contributed the land and the cost of erecting a building that was named Caruthers Hall and housed the law school for nearly 80 years.

From those Reconstruction years on, a great if poorly paid faculty was teaching the students in the College of Arts and Sciences, the Theological School, and the Preparatory School. The average length of service of a Cumberland teacher of this era was 43 years.

From scattered shabby buildings in the small town, a circumstance which led to much dissension, Cumberland slowly moved into adequate housing for its schools: Caruthers Hall (1877) for the law school; Divinity Hall (1866) for the theological school; Memorial Hall (1896) for the literary school; and the former Campbell Academy building for the preparatory school until 1902. (The theological school moved to Memorial Hall in 1896, the preparatory school in 1902, and from 1951 to 1955 the law school met there.)

Women students were admitted to Cumberland after 1897. The expedient of a contractual alliance with Lebanon College for Young Ladies (established in 1886) under the name "The Annex" had preceded the official acceptance of the new policy.

In 1906 the Presbyterian Church USA became the sponsor of the university. In 1909, as a result of litigation between the Cumberland Presbyterian Church and the Presbyterian Church USA, the theological school was closed. For one year the theological school classrooms and library were occupied by the Presbyterian Seminary of the South, an independently established school with a new charter, until its merger with Lane Seminary and removal to Cincinnati, Ohio. The relationship with the Presbyterian Church USA continued until 1944. From 1946 to 1951 Cumberland was operated under auspices of the Tennessee Baptist Convention. In the spring of 1951, after an attempt to remove the college to the newly acquired campus of Ward-Belmont College in Nashville had been successfully resisted, the operation of Cumberland was restored to its own independent board of trustees.

Changing conditions in higher education modified the program of the college. The school began deliberately to concentrate its efforts into a sphere in which it could use its limited resources to excel. In September 1956, after a five-year interim during which only the School of Law was operated, the Cumberland College of Arts and Sciences was reopened as a two-year liberal arts college. It is a member of the Southern Association of Colleges and Schools, the Tennessee College Association, and the American Association of Junior Colleges, with full accreditation. For a number of years Cumberland was the coordinating institution for the AAJC program with developing institutions

Named for Judge Robert L. Caruthers, Caruthers Hall housed the Cumberland University Law School from 1878 to 1962. Not only did such students as Cordell Hull, secretary of state, Nobel Prize winner, and US senator, attend classes here, but most of Lebanon's public programs, plays, revues, and lectures were presented in the auditorium.

in the Central South. Enrollment steadily increased and by 1970 it exceeded any previous number in the history of the college. An official enrollment of 505 in September 1980 was the highest figure of record. (For all of its schools, the university's greatest enrollment was 848, recorded in 1948.)

In 1961 the School of Law moved to the campus of Howard College (now Samford University) in Birmingham, Alabama. The removal was made necessary by the new requirements adopted by the Association of American Law Schools for approval, requirements which were far beyond the means of a small independent school. Efforts to retain the school within Tennessee were frustrated and the offer of Howard College was accepted. The following year saw an official change of name to Cumberland College of Tennessee and admission to full membership in the Southern Association, a goal long sought. Under the leadership of Edward Potter, David K. Wilson, and Athens Clay Pullias, successive chairmen of the board, and President Ernest L. Stockton, whose father had served as president of the university from 1927 to 1941, Cumberland moved into a development program that included an extensive program of construction and renovation, landscaping, strengthening of library and fine arts programs, and faculty development. In 1972 Bert Coble became a member of the faculty and under his direction Cumberland developed an attractive music program that led to a new Associate of Music degree. An honors program, directed by James Dressler, was instituted in 1980. In November 1981 the board of trustees authorized a return to four-year status with additional programs in allied health services, business administration, and communications to commence in September 1982.

The Gray and The Blue

They fought in a star-crossed cause. While the shocks of battle and the hardships of life behind the opposing lines swept their homeland, soldiers from Wilson County fought on every front, from Virginia to the Trans-Mississippi. They were in the infantry, in the cavalry, in the artillery, in the engineers, in the scouts, in the navies of the Union and of the Confederate States.

Six companies of the Seventh Tennessee infantry regiment were raised in Wilson County; one each in DeKalb and Smith; two in Sumner. The Wilson County companies left Lebanon May 20, 1861, having receiving their colors two days before from the hands of Miss Mary Cahal, niece of Robert L. Caruthers, former Congressman and justice of the Tennessee Supreme Court. The women and girls of the county had made their uniforms. Wagons and carts filled the Public Square and all the streets. Brass bands played. Bartlett Graves, a veteran of the War of 1812, piped the men in gray off to war. The volunteers reached Nashville in vehicles furnished by citizens of the county. Thomas Jefferson Holloway, one of those volunteers, wrote: "My country says my services are needed in her defense and I should feel myself recreant in my duty did I not submit without a murmur." Tom Holloway was to be killed at Gettysburg.

The companies were organized into a regiment at Camp Trousdale in Sumner County. The original officers were Robert Hatton, colonel; John F. Goodner, lieutentant colonel; John K. Howard, clerk and master of the chancery court of Wilson County and author of the Declaration of Independence of Tennessee adopted by the General Assembly on May 6, 1861, major; Monroe Anderson, Dr. J. A. Anthony, James Baber, Thomas H. Bostick, Clint Douglas, John A. Fite, Nathan Oakley, Samuel G. Shepard, W. H. Williamson, R. C. Wright, captains. In July 1861 the Seventh Tennessee left for Virginia. After the Cheat Mountain and the Bath and Romney campaigns in western Virginia the soldiers were ordered to the defense of Richmond in the spring of 1862. Hatton, newly promoted to Brigadier General, was killed in the Battle of Seven Pines. They fought in the Seven Days battles before Richmond, at Culpepper Courthouse, Second Manassas, Centreville, Bolivar Heights, and at Antietam (Sharpsburg) with the Army of Northern Virginia when part of A. P. Hill's Light Brigade saved the day there. The regiment fought again at Fredericksburg and Chancellorsville and Gettysburg. There it fired the first shot of the battle, lost the first man killed,

Confederate Monument, Lebanon, Tenn.   10006

Lebanon's best known landmark is the Confederate monument, a statue of congressman and General Robert Hatton, erected in 1912. General Hatton was killed at the Battle of Seven Pines in 1862.

and in charging up Cemetery Ridge took its Stars and Bars inside the Union line behind the famous stone fence. Afterward the survivors fought the rear guard action at Falling Water, the last battle of the army north of the Mason-Dixon line. In the Wilderness, Spottsylvania, Petersburg, the Weldon Rail Road, Fort Archer, and Appomattox (where 47 surrendered their arms and their flag at the orders of Robert E. Lee) the Seventh Tennessee earned fame.

In the fall of 1861 four more companies of infantry were raised and joined the 45th Regiment of Tennessee Infantry; during the same period three companies of cavalry were formed and became part of the Fourth Regiment of Tennessee Cavalry. There were substantial numbers of Wilson County soldiers in the 18th, 24th, 28th, 38th, and 45th Tennessee Infantry; the 2nd (or 22nd), 4th (Starnes-McLemore, also called the 3rd), 4th (Smith's, also called the 8th), and 5th Tennessee Cavalry; the 1st Tennessee Heavy Artillery, all Confederate States Army; as well as in the 5th (Stokes) Cavalry and 4th Tennessee Mounted Infantry regiments, United States Army. Some Wilson countians were in the 8th Texas Cavalry (Texas Rangers) and the 2nd Kentucky Cavalry of General John Hunt Morgan's command.

In many ways, Wilson County was a key to the strategic moves of both armies between the fall of Nashville in February 1862 and the advance toward Chattanooga in the summer of 1863. Twice, in August 1862 and in June 1863, a full-scale battle might have developed near Lebanon. As late as August 11, 1862, General Braxton Bragg intended to direct his offensive against Nashville from the direction of Lebanon. General Kirby Smith's success at Cumberland Gap altered Bragg's plans and he made his futile advance into Kentucky. During the spring of 1863 a flank attack on Union communications at Murfreesboro was constantly threatened by Morgan's substantial force around Liberty and was always feared by the Union command.

Days of significance to Wilson County included February 16, 1862, when Crittenden's army retreated from the east across the county; March 15, 1862, when Morgan's cavalry camped at Lebanon en route to Gallatin; March 22, 1862, when Lebanon was occupied by U.S. troops commanded by Lt. Col. Marcellus Munday; and May 5, 1862, when Morgan's men fought an action against U.S. cavalrymen on and around the Public Square of Lebanon. On July 20, 1862, Nathan Bedford Forrest's cavalry occupied Lebanon, disappointed in hopes of a battle with the 74th Ohio Cavalry, which had been stationed there but which had been warned and withdrew.

After the Battle of Perryville, Kentucky, both Union and Confederate armies withdrew south across the western part of the county and on November 9, 1862, there were skirmishes at Lebanon and Silver Springs. On November 15, Morgan encamped at Baird's Mill and on November 17 there was an action at Rural Hill. Morgan made a successful raid on Hartsville on December 6 with over 5000 infantry, cavalry, and artillery. A considerable number of irregular troops—sympathetic citizens who just picked up their guns and went along—accompanied the

Confederates, according to Union sources. Morgan returned through Lebanon with 2000 prisoners the next morning, all concerned being wet, muddy, and half-frozen.

From January to June 1863 Morgan was encamped around Liberty, and his cavalry was often in Wilson County. Lebanon was a center of espionage for both sides and of smuggling of medical supplies from Nashville into the Confederate lines. On January 21 there was a Federal reconnaisance to Cainsville; on January 29 Morgan attempted unsuccessfully to infiltrate Nashville by way of Stewart's Ferry; on February 15 there was a Federal reconnaissance to Cainsville and a skirmish. The Federal troops undertook a major expedition toward Liberty from February 17 to 20. A skirmish at Statesville on March 19 was further proof of the nervous sensitivity of the Union command toward the potential threat of Morgan's force. The expedition of 2500 Union soldiers under Col. John T. Wilder on April 1–8 was the most extensive operation, confiscating livestock and supplies and returning to camp at Murfreesboro with animals, prisoners, freed slaves, and information. Among the prisoners were eight Southern conscription officers and a mail carrier. Col. R. H. G. Minty took a cavalry brigade and marched through the same territory in the opposite direction (counter-clockwise) April 2–6. On April 6 Gen. Robert Mitchell with 400 cavalry and mounted infantry moved out of Nashville and surprised the Confederate conscripting camp at Green Hill. The Union army's fear was somewhat justified. On April 9 General Joe Wheeler came through Lebanon from Sparta and conducted a slashing attack on the railroad line near the Hermitage the next day.

On May 12–16 there was another Federal reconnaissance toward Liberty and Lebanon, based on Murfreesboro. A month later, on June 15, Colonel Minty led an expedition from Murfreesboro to Lebanon by way of Baird's Mill, where they found picket fire but no Confederates. Getting to Lebanon at 4 AM Tuesday, Minty could get no information at first but finally some sympathizers reported that Gen. Basil Duke (Morgan's brother-in-law) and 600 men had left by the Sparta road the day before. At Spring Creek a skirmish began that moved down the road to

Shop Spring, the Confederates fighting stubbornly from behind fences. By 2 PM the Union force reached Waters' Mill (Watertown), where it was learned that Morgan was at Alexandria with 4000 men and artillery. All afternoon the skirmish kept up. At night the Union soldiers were able to fall back to Murfreesboro by way of Baird's Mill. As the rear guard left Baird's Mill a strong body of Southern cavalry came into the place, but there was only an exchange of shots. Inadvertently Minty had stumbled into Morgan's northward move into Kentucky and Ohio. The dashing Kentuckian was gone, nevermore to be seen in Middle Tennessee.

Not until August 29, 1864, were there organized Confederate troops in Wilson County. Then Wheeler's cavalry, raiding in a wide circle from East Tennessee to Alabama, struck Union communications at Lebanon. In September Lebanon was finally evacuated by Federal soldiers. At some time after the Federal evacuation the handsome building of Cumberland University, its interior ravaged by occupying soldiers, the campus rutted and scored, was burned to the ground by Confederate soldiers, under command of an officer who had been a student at the school. Like the exact date, the regiment responsible has not been identified. It was perhaps part of Hood's army advancing on Nashville.

On May 26, 1865, James L. Barry and 25 other Smith and Wilson County soldiers who had surrendered in North Carolina walked into Lebanon from Murfreesboro, where they had been transported by train. The next morning there was the biggest flood that Lebanon had ever known: the water was nearly six feet deep on the Public Square. Barry, who lived until April 15, 1947, the last surviving veteran of the Civil War in Tennessee, said later: "Well, we went through Hell and high water but we got home."

A Fence at Gettysburg

"There was a sandstone fence right on top of the hill, Cemetery Ridge. When I crossed the last fence, the enemy was getting ready to fall back, seemed to be, but just after we crossed,

In 1899 members of the local chapter of the United Daughters of the Confederacy represented each Confederate state at the unveiling of the monument in Cedar Grove Cemetery. There were *(from left, first row)* Laura Lireland, Mary Harkreader, Alice Williamson, Porter McFarland, Buena Vista Doak; *(second row)* Birdie Gwynn, Nora Faulkner, Willie McFarland, Gertie Fakes; *(back row)* Martha Williamson, Mary Barbee, Hester McClain, Eudora McGregor.

a fresh command was put in on the Yankee side and what wasn't shot down of our crowd fell down."

In those words Colonel John A. Fite of Carthage and Lebanon described a turning point in American history. The day was July 3, 1863; the place was a college town in Pennsylvania. Well-blooded by two years of battle, the youths of the Seventh Tennessee Infantry from Wilson, Smith, DeKalb, and Sumner counties stepped briskly down the road from Cashtown to Gettysburg on July 1. They were part of General Archer's Tennessee Brigade, once Robert Hatton's, and it was one of the best in R. E. Lee's Army of Northern Virginia.

Shortly before noon on that July day the first shot of the Battle of Gettysburg was fired by the Seventh Tennessee as it encountered Reynolds' Corps of the Federal Army of the Potomac just outside the town. The first Confederate to fall was Henry Raison, a Sumner County soldier of Company B, Seventh Tennessee. On the next day the Seventh was not in action but on July 3 it was part of the great battle line that charged Cemetery Ridge under Pettigrew and Pickett.

"July 3 was the hottest day I think I ever saw," said Colonel Fite more than 60 years later as he sat in the cool shade of his daughter's front porch on West Main Street, Lebanon. "We had about a quarter of a mile to go, up a tolerably steep hillside, not a bush on it."

The Confederate columns moved forward under heavy fire from the heights controlled by the Union Army on that sultry July day. Colonel Fite led the regiment. There was a sandstone fence on top of Cemetery Ridge. Behind it were Federal soldiers and guns. The Confederate barrage had gone over their heads and the defense positions were intact. There were two fences along the Emmittsburg Road, both under pointblank cannon fire. Colonel Fite and a handful of others crossed the last fence. The colonel had been hit at Mechanicsville by a spent cannonball. He had been shot in the leg at Orange Court House. He had been shot in the stomach at Fredericksburg. And not even the greatest barrage of the campaign could kill him. He was captured by a Rhode Island artillery officer.

There at the farthest advance of the Southern Confederacy Captain A. D. Norris, a 26-year-old teacher, ripped the regimental flag off its staff and hid it beneath his coat. As he and other survivors stumbled back down the hill the brigade, which had lost two commanding generals during the battle, was under the command of Lt. Col. Sam G. Shepard of Gladeville, Wilson County. As Shepard got back to the Confederate artillery, General Lee stopped him, took his hand, and said: "The fault is mine, but it will be all right in the end." It was the end of the battle proper, but not the end of the action. As Lee's battered columns moved toward the Potomac, the Tennessee Brigade guarded the

rear. If the Federals could cut off the retreat, disaster would follow. At Falling Water, near Hagerstown, where Lee's troops were
crossing the Federal attack came. The Seventh held it off. It was
the last battle fought by the Army of Northern Virginia north of
the Potomac.

First, farthest, and last: the Seventh Tennessee Infantry Regiment fired the first shot and lost the first man, took its flag farthest, and fought the last skirmish of the battle that decided that
the United States of America would remain one nation indivisible.

The Fighting Parsons

There were in the Confederate States Army a remarkable
quartet of preacher officers. They were David Campbell Kelley,
John Dillard Kirkpatrick, Samuel George Shepard, and James
Madison Phillips. Two were Baptists, one was Methodist, one a
Cumberland Presbyterian. All were from Wilson County. All became famous, all survived the war, and all enjoyed long fruitful
careers in the ministry.

Colonel Kirkpatrick was second in command of General John
Hunt Morgan's raiders. When the Civil War began he was in charge
of Walnut Grove Cumberland Presbyterian Church near Gallatin. He organized a battalion of cavalry and became its captain.
During Morgan's Raid through Indiana and Ohio, Kirkpatrick's
was the only company which did not surrender with Morgan at
Buffington, Ohio. Instead he and his men crossed the Ohio River
in a boat, steered by the colonel, who was wounded during the
crossing. Returning to Knoxville, he was put in command of the
remnant of Morgan's men who had not joined the unfortunate
campaign and led them until Morgan, having escaped prison,
returned and Kirkpatrick was directed to report to him with his
800 men. After the war he returned to the ministry and in 1880
became a professor in the Theological School of Cumberland
University until his death in 1895.

David Campbell Kelley had a career that in some ways par-
alleled Kirkpatrick's. Born at Leeville (then called Kelley's Church
for his father, the Rev. John Kelley) on December 25, 1833, he
went as a missionary to China in 1852 but returned in four years

because of the illness of his wife. He was preaching in Alabama when the Civil War began and raised a company of cavalry at Huntsville. Reporting to Nathan Bedford Forrest at Memphis, he was made a major and just before the Battle of Shiloh was promoted to lieutenant colonel, commanding a regiment on the retreat to Corinth. Colonel Kelley played a particular role at the battles of Eastport, where cavalry captured transport craft; Johnsonville; Murfreesboro; Chickamauga; Brice's Crossroads; Harrisburg; Franklin; and Nashville, where he commanded a brigade (Rucker's). He had three horses killed, received three bullets through his hat and one through his overcoat, and three more in his saddle, but was never wounded. He preached every Sunday while in camp. Returning to the Methodist ministry, he also was president of a school for girls, author of several books, and in 1890 candidate for governor of Tennessee on a prohibition platform, an action which caused him serious problems with bishop and conference. He died in Nashville in 1909.

Matt Phillips was born on a farm at Baird's Mill in 1840. At the age of 21 he raised two companies of soldiers in Wilson County and took them into the Confederate Army. He became a major of cavalry, fought at Stone's River, and then served with Col. Baxter Smith's regiment under General Joe Wheeler at Chickamauga, the Georgia campaign to Atlanta, at Saltville, Virginia, and with General Joe Johnston in the last stand in the Carolinas. Becoming a Baptist minister after the war he followed that career for 40 years, during which he was never without a pastorate for longer than a week. He was for several years editor of the *Christian Herald,* a widely-circulated nondenominational religious journal and served as president of the Masonic Colleges at Hartsville and Lebanon. He died in 1911.

Colonel Shepard found a place in history at Gettysburg where he brought the survivors of the Confederate charge back down Cemetery Ridge and was reassured by General Lee himself. He was to live another 57 years, teaching, preaching, farming near his native Gladeville, representing Wilson County in the Constitutional Convention of 1870 and the General Assembly of 1871–1873. Born in 1830, Shepard was the oldest of the "fighting parsons." He began the study of law just before the outbreak of war but then recruited a company of soldiers near Baird's Mill and took them, as the Hurricane Rifles, into the Seventh Tennessee. Elected captain of Company G, he served with the regiment through all the campaigns of the Army of Northern Virginia and surrendered with Lee at Appomattox. Shepard is mentioned three times by name in D. S. Freeman's monumental study of command, *Lee's Lieutenants*. His subsequent success in politics exemplifies the influence of the returned Confederate veteran. In Wilson County, those who had served in Gen. Robert Hatton's regiment and brigade were so numerous that for sixty years county politics was virtually controlled by their power. (Shepard had been one of Hatton's captains, two others became judges, a fourth was county trustee, and another superintendent of schools.) However Shepard's main energies were devoted to the Baptist church and he served most of the congregations of the immediate region either as pastor or revival preacher. He died in 1917.

Landmarks of Faith

There have been about 250 distinct congregations of various Christian bodies in Wilson County. It is therefore impossible to include a historical sketch of each. But Wilson County has played a significant role in American religious movements. Some of these instances must be mentioned.

The first regularly organized church in the county is still active after 180 years and in its formative years played a major role in a truly significant development—the revival movement on the American frontier. The Rev. Dr. James Hall of North Carolina constituted Spring Creek Presbyterian Church at Center Hill as a congregation in the summer of 1801. It had been meeting since 1799. Center Hill, near Doak's Crossroads, had been known as "the Donnell settlement" and Donnells have been on the church roll since its establishment. It was a Donnell who became the first pastor, the Rev. Samuel Donnell. When the fervor of the revival movement shook religious conservatism west of the mountains, it shook this "Old School" church and split it. Much of the congregation went to the new Bethesda church nearby but the Rev. Samuel Donnell, a traditionalist to the end, stood firm for "order in worship." When the Cumberland Presbytery became a separate body, all of the Presbyterian churches of the region except three—Hodge's at Shiloh in Sumner County, Craighead's at Nashville, and Donnell's on Spring Creek—went into it.

Wilson County and Lebanon were for over a century the heart of Cumberland Presbyterianism. At least five and probably eight of the preachers considered "the fathers of the church" lived or had lived in Wilson County. In addition to Bethesda, influential congregations of the church included Big Spring and Sugg's Creek. The fourth meeting of Cumberland Presbytery, less than one year after its founding, was at Big Spring on March 19, 1811. The sixth meeting, on April 7, 1812, was at Sugg's Creek. The General Synod was constituted in 1813. Its second meeting was at Sugg's Creek on April 5, 1814. At this time the Confession of Faith of the church was adopted, after deliberations requiring the greater part of four days. Two of the four members of the committee submitting the draft proposal were Wilson countians, Thomas Calhoun and Robert Donnell.

The Lebanon Theological Seminary, a department of Cumberland University, was established in 1852 by action of the General Assembly of the Cumberland Presbyterian Church and the board of trustees of the university and began its work in the fall of 1853 under the professorship of Dr. Richard Beard. With the exception of the Civil War years, the seminary continued its work successfully until it was discontinued in 1908. A new institution, the Theological Seminary of the South, occupied its quarters in Memorial Hall by rental for one year before making an alliance with Lane Seminary of Cincinnati, Ohio. The Bachelor of Divinity degree was conferred by Cumberland University upon 436 graduates. Several became moderators of the church, others became board secretaries, missionaries, presidents or professors of colleges, or occupied prominent pulpits. The seminary was the scholarly and theological heart of the denomination. Robert Verrell Foster, professor of systematic theology from 1893 to 1909, was the most productive writer and his four major books were widely recognized.

Even before the formation of Cumberland Presbytery, the revival movement, stemming from the Great Awakening in the Middle and New England states, had brought the camp meeting into the Cumberland valley. At a Wilson County campground of the Methodists there originated a practice that became an essential part of revivialism to the present day. It was the practice of "calling mourners" to the "mourners' bench" and is now more commonly called "the altar call." Billy Sunday, Gypsy Smith, and Billy Graham were to use it through the decades with remarkable effectiveness, as did the evangelists who conducted notable meetings in Wilson County—Sam Jones, Gen. R. M. Gano, Walt Holcomb, the House-Wall evangelist crusade, the Dan and Jack Fogarty ministry. But it originated at Ebenezer campground on the Coles Ferry Pike four miles from Lebanon with a Methodist minister, the Rev. Valentine Cook.

Ebenezer is hardly remembered, almost lost in trees and bushes. It is Bethlehem Methodist church, on Highway 70 on Hickory Ridge, that is a well-marked shrine, with one of the most historically significant houses in Tennessee standing behind the neat white frame building on the hillside. In 1815 the meeting house stood about one mile south of its present location, facing a road that led northward from the old highway to Nashville. Nearby was the farmhouse of William Babb. It was in the Babb house that Bishop Francis Asbury, old and too feeble to leave his bed, presided over his last annual conference, in October of 1815. The log dwelling was given to the Tennessee Conference of the United Methodist Church in 1969 by the William Gwynn Waters family, was moved 1½ miles down the hill, and has been restored. Nella Eatherly of Lebanon stated that her grandmother, Chloe Fisher Atkinson, told her that her grandmother, Chloe Babb Guthrie, said that when she was 12 years old she carried water to the aged bishop while he was sick and staying with her family in the upstairs bedroom of their home. She recalled that the bishop's cabinet met with him in this room. Still too weak to go to the meeting house, Bishop Asbury (before departing on the journey to the East during which he was to die) preached a sermon to a large gathering under the giant oak trees which shaded the southern part of the dwelling.

In 1838 the Rev. John Kelley was minister at Bethlehem. His wife, Lavinia, was the guiding spirit of a Woman's Missionary Society, credited by the Tennessee Conference with being the first formally set up as an official organization in the Methodist Episcopal Church, South.

Wilson County was in the center of Sacred Harp singing, and there are tunes named "Lebanon" and "Wilson" as well as "Rome," "Nashville," "Cookeville," and "Knoxville." In 1824 a song book called Columbian Harmony was printed by William Moore of Lebanon, a musician whose most well known tune is "Holy Manna."

Revivalism continued to be a strong strain in American religion, and in 1899 a remarkable meeting was held in Lebanon. The Rev. B. F. Haynes, then pastor of the Lebanon Methodist Church, secured the services of the Rev. H. C. Morrison of Louisville, Kentucky, editor of the *Pentecostal Herald*, to assist him in a series of revival services. The response was great; over a hundred persons were converted and some claimed the "second blessing" or the "blessing of sanctification." In a few weeks, the Rev. J. C. McClurkan of Nashville assisted in another series of services in a tent at Horn Springs. Here hundreds more were converted and sanctified, and there was so much general interest that it was decided to erect a permanent shed-type shelter for annual camp meetings. Ten acres on what is now Oak Street in Lebanon, near the sulphur spring, were purchased from Jeff Dodson. A Pentecostal Alliance was organized (with Dodson, Thel Horn, Billy Martin, Dave Seagraves, Frank Stratton, Sam G. Stratton, and others as charter members) and the site named the Wilson County Holiness Camp Ground. After a 60 x 90-foot building was erected, an all-day meeting of dedication was held. In the spring of 1901 the first great annual camp meeting took place. Thousands attended the 10-day encampment, many from other states, and Lebanon was recognized as the center of the Pentecostal movement in the Upper South.

More than 75 years earlier the reformation movement led by Alexander Campbell and Barton W. Stone reached Wilson County. Again a nationally known preacher worked in the county; in 1823 Stone was passing through Middle Tennessee on the old Trousdale Ferry Pike and asked a lodging for the night at the home of John and Sarah Scobey. Before retiring, the guest asked the family to read from the Scriptures together and join in prayer, a custom the Scobeys had already followed. A discussion of religion began which lasted all night and in the morning Mr. Scobey invited Mr. Stone to remain another night. Neighbors were asked to come and join the discussion. Thus a congregation was formed which became Bethlehem Church of Christ, oldest of that faith in the county.

Elder E. A. Elam of Lebanon, who died in 1929, was one of the most distinguished ministers of the Churches of Christ. Editor, author, president of the Board of Directors of David Lipscomb College, he is said to have drafted the language used in deeds to many church buildings: "that in the event instrumental music, missionary societies, or any other question of teaching or practice concerning which the New Testament is silent should divide the congregation the property would be held by those opposing such use or teaching."

Two Wilson County preachers earned distinction as Baptist historians. Elder John Bond, who began his ministry with Smith Fork Baptist Church but served Union (Old Hurricane) Baptist Church as pastor for 39 years, in 1859 wrote *The History of Concord Association,* the authoritative source for early Baptist activity in Middle Tennessee. Elder John Harvey Grime's *The History of Middle Tennessee Baptists* brings the narrative half a century further. He was a prolific writer and published at least 40 brochures, tracts, pamphlets, and books during his 90 years of life. He was also elected the first moderator of the Wilson County Baptist Association in 1921.

Of international reputation is a third Wilson countian. Cyrus Ingerson Scofield, born in Michigan, was reared in Wilson County. He left at the age of 17 to join the Confederate Army, in which he served throughout the war. After Appomattox, Scofield went to St. Louis and worked his way through law school, then became active in Republican politics. President Grant appointed him United States Attorney for Kansas and Indian Territory in 1873. At 30 he was the youngest U.S. Attorney in the nation. Six years later, a drunkard, he was converted to religion. He became acquainted with the evangelist D. L. Moody and was led to become pastor of the Congregational Church of East Northfield, Massachusetts. There he completed his life's great work—the Scofield Reference Bible.

Country Life

Country villages and general stores, small churches and blacksmith shops, doctors on horseback, and neighborly visits were the heart of life in rural Middle Tennessee in the last part of the nineteenth century, but the institution that has lingered longest in memory is the one-teacher school.

One of the lost schools in the Tennessee hills is the old Pick-Up School, which is no more than a legend now and is remembered only by a handful who attended it. It is believed that the oldest of these pupils now living are Eddie Williams of Statesville and his sister, Mrs. B. D. Moore of Lebanon.

Mrs. Moore recalled: "How strange it seems with over 86 years behind me that I still love my childhood life on a farm where the mountainous hills were around us. Early mornings at the break of day it seems as if I am whisked back to childhood when I loitered in early fall, anxiously waiting for the possum grapes and the nuts to ripen. And in the winter I remember the big snows. We had no thermometer then to tell the temperature but we knew when the snow was many feet deep and the creeks and ponds frozen solid for good skating. Then I'd hear the old folks say, 'It's cold enough to freeze the horns off a billy goat.' You don't know how I did wish that it would get our old billy's horns for he often got to be mean when he saw us playing out in the snow.

"We didn't have close neighbors, but everybody knew each other for miles around. One could tell when folks were home by the smoke curling out of the chimney. It was good to visit, take pot luck with a neighbor for a day or night. Pa would put a big back log on the fire and then add the forestick with smaller pieces between. We always expected company and were glad to see folks come. I'd hear the old women say that a man was coming because the right side of their noses itched. Others said it would be a woman because it was the left side. I jumped about and said, 'I know children are coming because the end of my nose itches!' I was anxious to play. Oftentimes when the snow was deepest we could see a number of folks coming. Some cut sticks to use as a walking stick in the snow.

"There were no phones, no mail route nearby. When there was news good or bad it traveled to all the neighbors. If sickness of misfortune struck the whole neighborhood got busy to help. They cut wood, did chores, cooked, washed, ironed, nursed those who needed them. Pa bought a Doctors' Book and became a very good doctor when there were no others. He'd take Mother to any woman who needed a midwife's help."

The Auburntown Road from Statesville follows Smith's Fork through Pick-Up. The valley, with its fertile farms and the big creek with its surrounding hills, is as pretty a scene as any in Middle Tennessee. Pick-Up once had a flourishing store, owned by Ernest Chumbly, where one could buy almost anything needed. Nearby on the big creek was a water mill where people from far and near came to have a sack of corn ground into meal. Mrs. Moore remembered: "It was a beautiful sight to see someone riding straddle of a horse with a big white cotton sack full of corn behind him. This sack of corn was called a 'turn of corn.' The mill was owned by J. T. Williams and it was here he was hurt and died. Across the road from the mill was a pretty country home in a beautiful setting on several hundred acres of land. Newburn Davis owned this farm, and he gave a small lot to have Pick-Up School built. The lot was too small for the children to play on and they went onto George Hutchinson's land adjoining the school lot to play. The school was not graded. Among the teachers were Ruth Dement, Hannibal Jennings, Harry Mullinax, and W. B. Williams, who became a lawyer. Sunday School and preaching were held in the school house too.

Before the new Norene telephone exchange was connected in October 1959 J. M. Jones, former owner of the Norene Telephone Co., plugged a final call through the old switchboard.

"The school was equipped with two big zinc water buckets. Each had a tin dipper with a black wooden handle from which all the children drank. Water was carried from a spring across the creek. When there was a big rain, Smith's Fork became a small river and covered up the spring. Finally a well was dug near the school.

"Everyone knew how to unravel an old sock and wind it to make a good yarn ball to play with, and the children could jump rope or play different games until it was time to be called in for books."

The Black Community

Black people have played a significant role in the story of Wilson County, and Wilson County black people have played a significant role in American life. One in every six residents of Wilson County is black. Their story begins at the very beginning, when the first settlers arrived in Middle Tennessee.

On Page 1 of Volume I of Wills and Inventories in the vault of the county clerk, the list of the property of the late Robert Wynne's estate begins, "1 negroe man named James; 1 negroe man named Daniel; 1 horse and saddle . . ." The progress of the black people of Wilson County during the eighteen decades since this entry was written in 1802 is almost immeasurable.

In the early years, the agricultural economy of the county did not demand forced labor and those who did own slaves only owned one or two. By 1820, there were 5,923 slaves in a total population of 18,730. The highest percentage of black persons was recorded in 1860 when there were 8,235 black slaves in a total of 26,072, an increase to 31 percent. There were in addition a number of free persons of color, most of whom were skilled laborers. The rise of large farms, although not true plantations in the Deep South sense, accounted for the increase. In town there were personal servants, gardeners, waiters, porters, and the like. Others worked as operatives in the mills of Lebanon, particularly those manufacturing textiles; they were not slaves of the mill owners but were leased or hired on annual contracts. These contracts generally began on January 1 and ran until Christmas Day, the week after Christmas being recognized as the hiring season.

During the Civil War, black people had a role to play. There were black regiments in the Union army, which also considered slaves valuable sources of information. The Confederates were not willing to form black military units but a Wilson County black man, Tom Lancaster, was General John Hunt Morgan's personal body servant and Bill Sealey served with Colonel John Fite until the officer was captured at Gettysburg. A number of black men served under the Stars and Bars and maintained, even after the war, Confederate sentiments. Slaves were also used as manpower when mineral veins in Seven Mile Bluff on the Cumberland River north of Lebanon were worked to provide lead for the Southern armies. Thomas and Morgan Davis of the James Harvey Davis farm near LaGuardo were two who gained their freedom in service as Union soldiers. Their father, Andrew Davis, later to become a prominent black minister, remained on the plantation, saying, "I am going to stay right here. I believe I will get my freedom just as soon as you get yours." His feelings exemplified the paradox that confronts historians who deal with the period and the institution. Loyal to his master, feeling almost a part of the family, not discontented in slavery, he yet welcomed freedom with joy: "At last the winter clouds are breaking, the birds have begun their early morning song, the fertile fields begin to show signs of life," Andrew Davis said. "This was the happy dawn." Emancipation came by state action in February 1865.

Why is Wilson County important in black history? Here are a few of the reasons:

W. E. B. Dubois taught school in Wilson County when he was a young man. He is one of the best known American black writers.

Two of the original Fisk Jubilee singers were from Wilson County. They were Maggie Porter (Cole) and Thomas Rutling.

Maude Woodfork McElroy was a nationally known radio and television personality, and performed before audiences as large as 10,000 persons in her role of "Aunt Jemima."

George Wharton Winston, a captain of the 366th Infantry Regiment, who served in France in 1918, was one of the first black officers in the American Army.

W. M. Manier was the first black American Legionnaire to

Later to become a leader of the black community and a prominent funeral director, Ben T. Caruthers in 1921 was a young man in a two-horse wagon.

receive the Babe Steagall trophy for the best record of a service officer in work for veterans, their widows, and their orphans.

The lawsuit of *Clifford Theodore Sloan et al.* vs. *Tenth Special School District* in the United States District Court, heard September 18 and 19, 1963, before Judge William E. Miller for the purpose of extending the original suit to the schools operated by the Wilson County Board of Education after the original suit had resulted in the desegregation of Tenth District schools in 1961, was a landmark in Tennessee school desegregation cases, and orders in that case served as precedents and patterns for desegregation of the larger urban school systems throughout the state.

Generally the race relations record of Wilson County has been good, although some violence, including one twentieth-century instance of lynch law, has marred it. The Ku Klux Klan was never very active in the county after the Civil War. Although there was a unit of the modern Klan active in the 1920s, its energies appeared to have been directed at erring wives and drunken wife-beaters of the majority race. Perhaps because the local agent of the Freedman's Bureau, Dr. S. B. F. C. Barr, a native of Wilson

County, was tactful, understanding, and effective, harmonious
relations generally prevailed. Indeed in 1876 a black man, S.
Jordan, a shoemaker by trade, was elected a member of the Wilson County quarterly court.

Desegregation of the public schools, of public swimming pools,
of theaters and restaurants, of such public facilities as water
fountains and rest rooms was accomplished with a minimum of
friction although some marches and demonstrations occurred
during the 1960s. In the summer of 1964 James Bryant, principal of Wilson County High School, was employed as a teacher
in the county summer school at Lebanon High School. This was
the first integration of public school facilities in Wilson County
and was done prior to any federal court order. He later became
a member of the Lebanon High School faculty. In June 1970
William Kenneth Head, son of Mr. and Mrs. Marvin Head, received the Bachelor of Science degree from Fisk University, after
being the first black student to enroll in Lebanon High School.
The first basketball All-American at Cumberland College, Marvin Carr, was black. Manier, the first black member of the Lebanon Police Department, was nationally recognized by the
American Legion. In addition to the Steagall Award, he was the
first black Tennessean invited to the annual National Rehabili-
tation Conference and was named Legionnaire of the Year in
1972.

The last African-born family to come to Wilson County in
the days of slavery was brought to the farm of Alex Simmons
near Simmons Bluff in the 1840s. Mintus and Sylvia Simmons
and their two sons, Horace and Anthony, had been smuggled
into the United States, for the slave trade had been illegal for
more than 30 years, and came to Nashville. Six other children
were born in Wilson County and their descendants remain. Some
are named Price, for Horace took that name from Col. M. A.
Price, who acquired him in the 1850s. In Tennessee, slaves used
the master's surname and many noted Wilson County names are
now borne only by black persons who bring new credit to them.
They include Stokes, Caruthers, Crutchfield, McGregor, Wharton, Richmond, Bender, Head, Hurd, Logue, Moxley, Muir-

head, Officer, Owens, Pennington, Provine, Rhone (Roane), Rhodes, and Settles.

The New South in Wilson County

The years from 1890 to 1920 are sometimes called the Progressive period of American history. Social, economic, political, and cultural life was in ferment. In literature the movement was called Naturalism; in politics there were various forms of socialism. In the South agrarian Populism attracted many followers (both the National Grange and the Farmers Alliance were influential in Wilson County) somewhat earlier than 1890 and the movement often expressed passionate opposition to industrialism, which was seen as a form of exploitation by northern capitalism. Proponents of industrial development called their movement by various names. The most widely accepted was "The New South."

Wilson Waters' Dream

Wilson Lawrence Waters was one of those movers and shakers that the nineteenth century produced. He was born November 11, 1818, married Christiana Bryan, became a merchant at Three Forks, the community at the confluence of the three streams that formed Round Lick Creek, and trained himself to be a construction engineer. He then became a leader in the formation of the Lebanon & Sparta Turnpike Company, which constructed a new road to replace the old stagecoach road (sometimes called Walden Ridge Road). While operating a farm of 400 acres on the eastern side of Round Lick Creek, he built in 1857 a grist mill across the turnpike from his store. The post office had been moved to the store in 1845 and the name changed from Three Forks to Watertown. The village until 1885 was no more than the store, post office, blacksmith shop, grist mill, saw mill, the Waters house, a stately two-story white frame dwelling with green shutters, and a few small houses across the creek. But Wilson Waters' dream was about to become reality.

He had been a Whig and a slaveholder but freed his people

before 1860. In 1856, a supporter of the new Republican party, he attended its national conventon and again attended in 1860. There were many Unionists in DeKalb and upper Wilson counties and his position was not untenable during the Civil War; he remained a Republican, ran unsuccessfully for Congress in 1865, and was elected to the state General Assembly in 1865 and 1867.

Still president of the turnpike company, Waters was one of the organizers of the Wilson and Allen Foundry in Nashville. With his son-in-law, Dr. R. H. Baker, and others he brought the route of the new Nashville & Knoxville Railroad through Watertown, which later became part of the Tennessee Central system. The village more than doubled in size. In 1903 a disastrous fire leveled the central part of the town. At a called meeting of citizens, $800 was subscribed to buy the lots made bare by the flames and a large public square was developed, surrounded by store buildings of brick and stone and, after incorporation in 1905, a city hall. In 1921 a large brick school building replaced a wooden structure and in 1929 a new building for the high school rose. Subsequent expansion, remodeling, and new construction have given Watertown and the 16th civil district excellent facilities for education. But Wilson Waters did not live to see this growth of which he had dreamed, for on December 3, 1903, he died.

Industry assisted in giving the community vitality—principally the W. E. Stephens Manufacturing Company, but also Wilson County Garment Company, the Carnation Company, Williams Manufacturing Company which in 1928 was operating the world's largest wooden pin mill at Watertown, and Moers Mills. Automobile dealerships opened at an early date; Dr. W. J. Winter operated the first automobile in the area in 1905. On March 23, 1909, an automobile line began service from Watertown to Smithville and the last section of the once-prosperous Sparta-to-Nashville stagecoach line was suspended. In 1912 Elby Jennings and the American Hardware Company had the first Ford agency in Watertown.

In 1970 a new water plant, designed by J. R. Wauford, was called the most modern in Tennessee. But although the average municipal indebtedness in the state increased 75 percent from

Until the 1920s, when trucks and better highways were available, poultry and livestock were driven to market on foot. This large flock of geese is pausing on the Public Square of Watertown before continuing on to Nashville.

1960 to 1970 Watertown's net direct debt declined 47 percent, from $25,000 in 1955 to zero in 1965 and to $9,452 in 1969. In 1980 a $50,000 Community Development grant, totally funded by the U.S. Department of Housing and Urban Development was recommended.

When the Lights Came On

The coming of electric lights to Lebanon on a certain night in 1890 is within the memory of a few elderly Wilson countians. The whole Mount View neighborhood gathered at the school to see the lights go on for the first time. Few places command as good an overview of the county seat, and when J. J. Hatcher, the first city electrician, pushed the switch and what must have looked like a myriad of fireflies illuminated the gathering dark a great gasp was heard from those who had known only the candle and the oil lamp.

For many of the farm families of Wilson County it would be another half century before the power lines reached their houses and their barns, when among other accomplishments of the New Deal rural electrification programs became reality.

Not many nights after the gathering at Mount View school, young Dixon Merritt, then not quite 12 years old, was taken by his Uncle Pat Henderson downtown to see the place where electricity was made. Many years later he remembered it. Then he said: "I was spending a few days with my Aunt Evelyn in Lebanon, and her husband was going mainly to buy a red snapper steak at John Trebing's meat market, but he also wanted to show his country nephew the city sights. It was near the spring in the northwest corner of the Square on the west side, I believe, in the building where the shoe shop is—that, or the one where the barber shop is (the Coaplen Building). I can still see the big wheel turning and Jeff Hatcher working around with the mysterious stuff that could kill a man as easily as it could light a lamp."

That Wonderful Year—1908

That was the year that was, that wonderful year, 1908. For Lebanon may have been founded in 1802 and chartered in 1819 but modern Lebanon traces its birth to 1908.

Industry, destroyed by the Civil War and Reconstruction, returned that year. Good water from artesian wells replaced the contaminated water from the historic Town Spring in Lebanon faucets. Users of electricity found their bills lower. It was a dramatic year which epitomized the spirit of The New South.

The year began with the trial of the slayer of young Alvin Jenkins of Dodoburg, a trial that required examination of 600 prospective jurymen. In February, there was the climax of the great Melvin lot swindle. Many prominent citizens of Wilson County had been sold lots in a mythical Oklahoma "town" by a confidence man. When the swindler was arrested, Walter Hancock agreed to act as prosecuter. After a long trial, the jury failed to agree.

Politics reached fever pitch in the election of a governor. The rival candidates, Senator Edward Ward Carmack and Governor Malcolm Patterson, conducted one of a series of joint debates in Lebanon. Thousands heard them after an impromptu parade

The residence of Herman Cox, employee of the Lebanon Woolen Mills, stood in the lane adjoining the mill beside other workers' houses. He and his family are standing on the porch in 1914.

of cheering Carmack supporters escorted the carriage of their favorite through the streets. It was this campaign that led directly to the year's biggest sensation. On June 22 a Nashville newspaper published a letter from Lebanon dealing with the political campaign. The letter mentioned the name of Captain Ellis Harper of Lebanon, a former state official and a guerrilla fighter of the Civil War. Harper discovered who had written the letter. It was Bill Suite of Lebanon. When Harper went to chastise the writer, there were shots and the one-time Confederate raider, a friend of Frank and Jesse James, lay dead on the ground. It was the morning of July 25, 1908. Less than four months later, Senator Carmack, whose fiery oratory had created the atmosphere that led to Harper's death, lay dead himself of a pistol shot on a Nashville sidewalk.

In 1902 the first Tennessee Central train came from Harriman into Nashville. For the first time Lebanon and Wilson County were on a main line, and not only could rail transportation bring products in, but produce of Wilson County farms and factories could be sent east and west. On May 28, 1908, the organization of the Lebanon Woolen Mills was announced. On August 20, the Nashville, Chattanooga & St. Louis Railroad, which had operated its Lebanon Branch short line since 1877 when it acquired the 30 miles built by the ambitious planners of the Tennessee & Pacific, announced it would bring its tracks from the old depot a mile south of the Public Square into a new station in the downtown area at the corner of East Gay and South Cumberland streets. On August 27 the Gulf Red Cedar Company announced it would bring its pencil block manufacturing plant to Lebanon. The industrial growth of this farm market town was assured.

On July 1 Lebanon became eligible for free city mail delivery. Consequently houses were numbered for the first time. New sidewalks were to be laid wherever the letter carrier was to give service. Planning for a new post office building (completed in 1914) was begun. Congress passed Representative Cordell Hull's bill providing money for this new federal building.

Meanwhile Cumberland University received the first encouraging news since the controversy between two bodies of Presbyterians put its future in jeopardy. The U.S. Court of Claims ruled favorably on its claim against the U.S. government for damages for the burning of the university building on South College Street in 1864. The money received was sufficient to keep financial affairs manageable and may even have assured the continued operation of the school. More frivolous but still encouraging was the southern championship in basketball won by the Cumberland team in 1908.

"There is a spirit of civic improvement pervading the atmosphere," observed *The Lebanon Democrat* in September. By that time the new Bank of Mt. Juliet had opened for business; the Lebanon mayor and aldermen had cut the cost of electricity from the new power plant to eight cents a kilowatt; and the Town Spring had been abandoned. This last act was a significant symbol of the new day. For more than a century Lebanon had liked and used the water from the spring where Neddy Jacobs had settled. At last it became obvious that typhoid fever lurked in the bubbling stream. Down went the drills through the limestone and by mid-1908 the new artesian wells and the standpipe for storage were ready. Almost sadly the town closed down the pumps at the old Town Spring. Into the pipes went the well water. Gone were the otters and the muskrat, gone the buffalo and the deer, gone the arrow and the long rifle. The new day had dawned.

Over the Top: The First World War

On April 6, 1917, President Wilson called for a declaration of war against Germany. That spring a tent was erected on the south side of the Public Square in Lebanon for recruiting volunteers. In charge was John Fite Robertson, newly appointed a second lieutenant by Governor Tom Rye and wearing a brand new officer's uniform bought at Burk & Company in Nashville. That was the beginning of Company B, 2nd Tennessee Infantry. On August 13 the company was ordered to Nashville under command of Capt. John H. "Honus" Craig with Robert M. Gray of Fayetteville first lieutenant and Robertson second lieutenant. On September 10 the regiment entrained for Camp Sevier, South Carolina, to become a part of the 30th Infantry Division. In September the regiment was broken up and the officers and men were reassigned, some to the 115th Field Artillery, including Lt. Robertson, some to the 117th Infantry, and some to the 119th Infantry. The division embarked for France in May and June 1918, and the 119th took an active part in breaking the Hindenburg Line in northern France.

First Lt. Avis T. Hobbs went to France with the 30th Division. Promoted from private to lieutenant, he received the Distinguished Service Cross for brilliant action in the front line at Voorlezeele, Belgium, and Busigny, France, and was also decorated for valor by France and Belgium. It was the highest decoration received by a Wilson County soldier.

Sergeant Robert Burkett had been serving in the Philippine Islands for six years by 1917. He had been a private in the Spanish-American War and enlisted in the 7th Infantry regiment in 1901. Soon after the declaration he was on his way to France.

During the war he served with the 26th Infantry regiment of the 1st Division at the Marne, Chateau Thierry, and the Argonne. In 1929 he retired from active duty and returned to Wilson County.

Ross Neal was with the 6th Regiment of U.S. Marines in the St. Mihiel salient one Sunday morning about the middle of September 1918. They had been over the top once that morning, had returned, and were ready to go again. Noting that Neal's sharpshooting medal made a shiny target, an officer told him to put it in his breast pocket with his New Testament. The Marines advanced. A German shrapnel shell burst among them. Neal was showered from head to foot with fragments and was knocked unconscious. His pocket New Testament was found with an inch-long piece of shrapnel embedded in it, bending the medal behind it.

The most unusual service was required of Lee Whited and Capt. (later Colonel) Lewis Pendleton. Both served in Siberia where American troops were sent after the Russian Revolution. Whited was with the same 7th Infantry in which Sergeant Burkett had been serving at the outbreak of hostilities. It was October 1919 before Captain Pendleton returned home.

Edward Bringhurst stayed in France after the war, worked with the Peace Commission, and married a Frenchwoman before returning to America. In 1939 when war came to Europe again he was visiting in France.

Wilson County sent three companies to France, 46 men were wounded, and 20 died. Ten were killed in action: 1st Lt. Merrill Blanchard, 2nd Lt. Clyde O. Bratten, Pvt. John Davis, Pvt. Shelby Johnson, Pvt. Willie P. Moss, Sgt. Arthur Rodgers, Pvt. Alfred Shehane, Pvt. Jeff Washburn, Pvt. Jack Williams, and Pvt. Gordon Wynne. Ten others died in service, most of pneumonia. They were Pvt. Edward Ashworth, Cpl. Chester D. Crittenden, Pvt. Mental Dockins, Pfc. Shellie Hunter, Cpl. William F. Jackson, Pfc. Elder Jarrett, Pfc. John H. McCathrion, Pvt. William C. Marks, Pvt. Willie W. Pack, and Pvt. Mint Simmons.

There were 785 Wilson countians in service, including 21 Army officers, 6 Navy officers, 6 Marines, 73 sailors. The November

1918 Selective Service call required 179 men, who were never inducted. On November 11 a group of DeKalb County draftees arrived at Watertown to entrain. The news of the Armistice had been received by the time they got to the depot and they were sent home.

Every morning at 6 o'clock for almost 43 years David Upham Thompson of Watertown raised the American flag on a pole outside his home. The flag was a tribute to his son, Cpl. Joseph Thompson, who died in the Argonne in October 1918. When the father died at the age of 94 in June 1961, the flag was flown at half-staff.

When the American Legion was organized at St. Louis in May 1919, John Fite Robertson was one of the 22 Tennesseans who went from Nashville to attend the first caucus. Robertson was a member of the committee on resolutions. Immediately upon his return to Lebanon he obtained a subscription list of about 25 ex-servicemen and forwarded it to the national headquarters, receiving a charter for Wilson County Post 15. The name was later changed to honor Lt. Clyde O. Bratten, who was killed in action soon after the Hindenburg Line was broken.

Years of Promise, Years of Shadow

The 1920s did not roar in Wilson County or Lebanon. Rather the decade from 1919 to 1929 moved to the sound of the phonograph, the radio, the movie house, and the automobile, the cheering of spectators at athletic contests, and conversation about the stock market, real estate in Florida, and women's fashions.

The towns grew, principally the county seat where ditches were dug for a sewer system, streets were paved, and a reservoir built. Lebanon was already a school town. It became more so as Cumberland law school grew beyond all dreams—law students sought room and board among the townspeople and cosmopolitan accents were heard everywhere.

I'll Meet You at Shannon's

For three generations Shannon's Drug Store was the place where friends met. Between the World Wars it was virtually the

In 1920 this elephant escaped from the Robbins Brothers circus and led the citizens of Lebanon a merry chase before it was captured and taken to the county jail where Sheriff E. S. Bowers held it in custody.

center of community life. At 148 Public Square, in a building which had previously housed the E. D. Stiles drug store, customers and passers-by enjoyed refreshments, bought prescriptions and patent medicines, or received friendly greetings from the proprietors.

When he was only 13 years old, J. L. Shannon began to work in a drug store at Sharon in West Tennessee. He had been born and reared south of Lebanon. Later moving to Greenfield he sent his children back to Lebanon to school and in 1909 his son Homer Shannon got a job while still in school, helping to fill prescriptions in the D. Stiles store. In 1912 the father sold his Greenfield business and on September 28 opened a store in Lebanon. He and another son, Harry B. Shannon, were the registered pharmacists. Homer served in the Army and in 1921 the father took both sons into partnership under the firm name of J. L. Shannon & Sons. After his death the name was retained.

"Big Mister" (Harry) and Homer established a tradition of hospitality for young and old, city people and country folk, high school, college, and law student, and, during the Second Army maneuvers of 1942–1944, for the thousands of soldiers who crowded into the marble-floored aisle between candy, cigars, and perfume on the cash register side of the store and the soda fountain opposite. Some reached the two green-painted booths and the five or six marble-topped, wire-legged tables at the rear. It was said that Homer and Harry never refused to cash a check for a law student and that they never lost by doing so. Years later lawyers in every part of the United States would ask visitors from Lebanon, recalling their student days, about Shannon's. In 1972 William M. Cotton, Class of 1924, by then a successful magazine publisher, wrote:

"Remember the sound of a wooden stick run along the bars of an old iron fence at night on the way to your rooming house? Remember talking up for your opinions of the moment—loud and clear and hot—lounging around Shannon's fountain? Remember the fraternity houses and all their rivalries, important back then—and the sudden decisions to knock off the books and take yourself down to the soda fountain for a cold glass? Remember the back room? Remember your best friends of those days? Did you wish college days would never end?"

In 1937 George Tucker listed in his nationally syndicated column, "Man About Manhattan," the most mouth-watering delights of his experience and said, "It means particularly the ice cream sodas in Shannon's Drug Store in Lebanon, Tennessee."

The store's curb service during the late 1920s and 1930s stirred earnest rivalry from the adjoining Independent Drug Company. One particular summer clerks from the two stores vied strenuously to reach incoming cars first and to guide them into parking spaces in front of their respective establishments.

On February 10, 1968, Homer Shannon died at the age of 75 and was buried in Cedar Grove cemetery. He had been more than a business man, he had been a civic leader, a friend to the stranger in town, an institution. He was an organizer and a past president of the Lebanon & Wilson County Chamber of Commerce, a trustee of Cumberland University, a charter member of the Lebanon Rotary Club, a charter member and past commander of Clyde O. Bratten Post 15, the American Legion, and a member of the First Presbyterian Church. Born in Weakley County, he had come to Lebanon as a student, graduated from Castle Heights School and attended Cumberland where he had been a star baseball player. Both Homer and Harry Shannon were lifelong baseball fans, and Shannon's was the local headquarters for the World Series every fall. A radio at the rear of the store was tuned to the broadcast, the score by innings was painted on the front window for those standing outside and passing by, and another scoreboard was drawn in chalk mix on the large mirror on the back wall for fans seated and standing inside. "Big Mister" was happiest when the New York Yankees were participating. During football season the scores were drawn on the front window in white or pink chalk mix (used at other times to publicize "specials") as they were broadcast Saturday afternoons.

Three factors contributed to the decline of this social institution: the reduced enrollment and eventually the removal of the Cumberland law school, television, and the general vanishing of Saturday as market day. When the county courthouse was moved away from the Public Square in 1969 it was the end, almost the finish of the spirit of community but certainly of Shannon's as an institution.

In 1964 Homer, Harry, and their sister Mary were listed in the city directory, but Nick W. Powers of Memphis and Robert E. Daniel of Lebanon were shown as operators of Shannon Drug Company. In September 1964 Hardie Sorrells moved to Lebanon and purchased the store. By 1973, Sorrells having in the meantime acquired the Medical Arts Pharmacy on the corner of South College and East Gay streets, the prescription department of Shannon's was moved to the Medical Arts building but the old location remained as a luncheon counter, magazine stand, and store for the sale of sundries. In 1976 the store on the square was closed.

The Decade Ends

Representative of the 1920s in the county was the year that ended it, 1929. The promising prospects of the postwar years seemed near fulfillment, but as New Year's Day 1930 arrived there were shadows.

The year brought a new city charter and a new city administration for Lebanon, a new management for Castle Heights Military Academy under the auspices of the capitalist publisher Bernarr Macfadden, the largest number of law students Cumberland University had known up to that time, a new bridge in construction over the Cumberland River with the likelihood that the Chicago-to-the-Gulf Highway would cross it and pass through Lebanon, and in October a collapse in the stock market following the most prosperous twelve months of the first third of the twentieth century, among other events.

Macfadden believed fervently in physical education, not only for the young but for everyone, and his magazine, *Physical Culture,* was internationally known. Castle Heights moved into competition in athletics on a nationwide scale. In February 1929 the basketball team toured the North and in 10 days won four out of five games, including a victory over the U.S. Military Academy plebes at West Point. In April, Harry L. Armstrong was selected president of the academy, succeeding W. F. Godson. In September the school enrolled nearly 200 students, the largest enrollment since its founding in 1902. During the previous 10 years Castle Heights had never had more than 50 cadets in any single term.

The political developments in Lebanon were in every sense a milestone. The election of Frank Buchanan as mayor under the newly amended charter, which altered the municipal form of government from commission to council (mayor and board of alderman), expressed the deep dissatisfaction reflected in an editorial by Walter S. Faulkner appearing in *The Lebanon Banner* on October 3. He wrote:

> It is urgent that some changes be wrought or we rot. We have stood stock still in our tracks for nearly two full decades. Only our schools

A typical lawyer's office of the 1920s, the quarters of Walter S. Faulkner overlooked the Public Square directly opposite the courthouse. Through the open window he could hear the constable's cry summoning him to court.

and the university have shown any signs of healthy growth. Our water supply depends upon artesian wells which each summer threaten to be depleted so that even the gardens cannot be watered. Our deplorable record of destructive fires, fought with equipment purchased in 1914, forces insurance rates to prohibitive heights. It is impossible to ascertain the bonded indebtedness of the City of Lebanon with any accuracy because of the method used by the auditors. Even the names of bond holders do not appear to be of record in the City Hall.

The voters elected Buchanan and his ticket: Albert Buhler, Walter Ferrell, and Kerley Wilson. It was a crucial decision, and within two years new fire-fighting equipment had been bought and pipes were being laid toward the Cumberland River to assure Lebanon of an adequate supply of water for the foreseeable future.

County politics provided another memorable contest, the race between Frank McDaniel, incumbent county court clerk, and Curry O. Dodson. McDaniel had been elected to the office in 1917. Dodson, engaged in banking, was a young veteran of the World War newly returned to Lebanon after the collapse of the Florida land boom which had taken him, like so many Wilson countians, to that state. Both Dodson and McDaniel had extensive family connections, always important in county politics. Indeed, the Dodson forces prepared a large handbill headed "Ninety-Nine Years in One Family!" which accused kin and descendants of Josiah McClain of having monopolized the clerkship since 1831, except for the brief periods when Abraham Britton held it (1880–1882 and 1886–1890). In fact, Josiah and R. P. McClain, Jesse F. Coe, W. M. Harkreader, Harry Coe, and Frank McDaniel, who held the office in that order, were kin by blood or marriage. McDaniel won a narrow victory in August 1929; four years later he yielded the office to Dodson. Another political note of the year was the decision of Laura (Mrs. John) Mason (later Sanders) not to ask reelection as sheriff. Her chief deputy, Ed Climer, was nominated in August, to take office in September 1930. Mrs. Mason had succeeded to the office upon the death of her husband in 1926. She was reelected in her own right in 1928, one of the first women to be elected sheriff in the United States.

The courts disposed of several celebrated cases during the year. One was litigation which grew out of the attempted merger and subsequent liquidation of the Bank of Watertown and Citizens Bank, cases which became landmarks in the law of banking. Settled out of court in due course were lawsuits related to Castle Heights Military Academy: in one Colonel Godson sued Macfadden for breach of contract after his dismissal as headmaster and in another George V. Donnell charged Col. L. L. Rice of inducing him to invest in the academy by misrepresentations allegedly made when Rice disposed of his interest to a syndicate of Lebanon business men.

Industrial and commercial development were the objectives of other actions. Some of the political discontent was founded on a belief that the Lebanon Woolen Mills and its stockholders and management were systematically blocking the location of other industry in Lebanon. *The Lebanon Banner* made this thinly veiled charge on April 11 under the headline, "Why Are We Thus Deserted?" However, the commencement of construction of the new highway bridge at Hunter's Point on May 6 and a decision by the state to change State Highway 24 to a more direct route between Lebanon and Carthage, bypassing Bellwood and Rome, were considered promising moves for future growth.

In agriculture, still Wilson County's leading source of income, the Jersey cow was the symbol of prosperity. The importation in February of a herd of purebred Jersey cattle by Charles Williamson made his Green Hills Farm a center of attention. The 42 Jerseys were purchased in the Channel island in December and arrived at the farm on February 12, accompanied by Henry White, managing partner. These were the first imported Jerseys in Wilson County but there had been purebreds of the breed in the county since the 1880s. Edgar Waters of Greenwood Farm brought Buttercup, a famous cow, to be his foundation dam and this herd, operated successively by Lindsley, E.K., and Henry Waters, was one of the outstanding herds in America. Other registered Jersey breeders were John and Edgar Curd, T. S. Dillon, and John C. Sanders.

It was the year of the deep snow (15 inches on the ground at dawn February 21), a wet spring, and a dry fall. It was a year when the boyish look in women's fashions was on the way out. It was the year of the new small dollar bill and the new small automobiles—Marquette, Pontiac, Erskine, and Plymouth. Manager John Hatcher announced that the talkies were coming to his theater.

The new city administration announced its selection of officials. William Green would be city judge, Robert P. Gann chief of police, George Massey and Lynch Harris, sergeants, W. D. Ferrell, treasurer, James Babb, sexton of Cedar Grove cemetery, J. H. Cason, street superintendent, and Sam Stratton Bone, light and power department manager. Curry Dodson was to be clerk after all, but city clerk rather than county, and L. K. Odom was his assistant.

The stock market collapse of October was noticed only by the few wealthy enough to speculate in stocks. There were some tremors in the banking community as the American Banks of Nashville took over the Lebanon Bank & Trust Company and the knowledgeable worried a little about certain aspects of the operations of Caldwell & Company. But the 1930s were still in the future.

Depression and Recovery

In the 10 years that followed the Crash nationwide forces shaped life in Wilson County, although the kind of hardship and joblessness that afflicted the industrial North and Middle West and the Dust Bowl passed Middle Tennessee by. There were people out of work, farm prices were low, and many a morning a family man would listen desperately for the sound of the whistle at the Lebanon Woolen Mills, the major employer of the town, summoning hands to work. But the presence of Cumberland University, which offered a professional education at low cost and in a short time, brought needed cash into the economy. The hard times, the Bank Holiday of 1933, the election and inauguration of Franklin Delano Roosevelt, the "Fireside Chats" inspiring confidence, the Blue Eagle, the veterans bonus, AAA payments, the coming of rural electrification and TVA, and the creation of the Cedar Forest, a project of reclamation and reforestation almost symbolic in its channeling of energy into hope for the future, led the people from shadow into sunlight.

The Judge

The calm, imperturbable voice of Edward Glenn Walker spoke for Wilson County during hard times and recovery. Some swore by him; some swore at him; all acknowledged that he was a leader. Physically he was a big man. When he stood to open a meeting of the county quarterly court he loomed over the large room and dominated it, speaking softly but in a deep voice that allowed no

In 1931 a new bus station was opened by J. Edgar Evins and the Consolidated Bus Lines. It remained in this location for 15 years, serving thousands of passengers including many Wilson Countians who commuted regularly to work in Nashville.

misunderstanding. In 1915 he was elected county judge, a newly created office replacing the annually elected county chairman, and remained in that office until his death in 1940. He was elected president of the County Judges Association of Tennessee in 1939, and at the time of his death he had the longest tenure of any judge in the state. He lacked six months of attaining the required age to hold the office when first elected, but kept that fact a secret until after he had won election a second time. The most serious challenge to Judge Walker's administration was a result of the Depression in a way. In 1933 Walter Rose, a well-qualified member of the quarterly court, ran against Walker on an economy and low tax platform. Supporters of the challenger asserted that the incumbent was not counting the taxpayers' pennies in a time of economic hardship for farmers and land owners. His defenders pointed to the judge's dispensation, often quite unofficial, of charity to the needy and to his warm heart, as well as to the progress made in the county, not the least having been the removal of toll gates from the highways. Walker won 3501 to 2374.

The Writers

But the true sense of the times was furnished by the writers, particularly Dixon Merritt, Bowen Ingram, Paul Wooten, Terence Fugate, and L. L. Rice. Merritt, a newspaper and magazine editor, president of the Tennessee Press Association and of the American Press Humorists Association, was author of the well-known limerick about the pelican but he took more pride in the eight-volume history of his state, *Tennessee and Tennesseans,* on which he collaborated with Will T. Hale, a native of Liberty, in an authoritative history of the U.S. Department of Agriculture, and in "Our Folks," a signed, syndicated editorial column that accurately captured the flavor of the 1920s and 1930s. Merritt said that Wilson County offered her writers a good setting—better than the metropolitan restlessness of New York City and Washington where he had also worked, for there was an element of leisure, a certain letting-alone, and tolerance if not understanding.

Bowen (Mrs. Daniel T.) Ingram in her first novel, *If Passion Flies,* published in 1945, reproduces with warm and compassionate accuracy life in a Middle Tennessee town which she calls Meroville. There is little doubt that it is her home town and that its major characters are a composite of Lebanon people. The novel was followed in 1954 by *Light As the Morning,* whose narrator, Les, is a young boy trying to win a city tennis championship. Her third novel, *Milbry* (1972) went into three printings. Several chapters appeared first in the *New Yorker* and *Town & Country* magazines. The spirit and reality of a Middle Tennessee family and of a young girl growing up in the South in the time before the first World War are delicately captured.

Wooten, a writer of both prose and poetry, was published in leading magazines including the *Saturday Evening Post* and the

Ladies Home Journal during the 1930s and 1940s. Several of his poems were included in anthologics.

Fugate attended Castle Heights Military Academy and preserved his school days in a novel called *Drum and Bugle* (1961), a best seller that was reviewed nationally and went rapidly into paperback. Although scandalous in tone and resented by some, the novel does have at least some of the features of its models in its picture of MacFarland Military Academy and Cedarton as his hero Carl Roundtree saw them.

Laban Lacy Rice, president of both Castle Heights and Cumberland at widely separated times, tried his versatile hand at fiction writing on two or three occasions and in *Our Town, U.S.A.* (1962) depicts a small Tennessee town of the 1930s whose principal industry is the Mortimer Woolen Mills, whose governing body is a mayor and council, and where there is a small but distinguished private college. Lebanon residents enjoyed this opportunity to guess at real identities and to speculate whether the fictional incidents had a basis in reality.

Mrs. Ingram's sister, Virginia Prewett Mizell, held the widest international reputation as a writer. A political reporter for the *Chicago Sun* in Latin America during the late 1930s, she wrote *Reportage on Mexico* (1941) and *Beyond the Great Forest* (1953) in addition to her articles for the *Sun* and the *Washington Post.* In 1945 she received Brazil's highest honor, the Order of the Southern Cross, for her coverage of the Chapultepec Conference.

At an earlier time a former resident of Wilson County, Cale Young Rice, brother of Laban Lacy, had become one of the major American poets. During the first decade of this century he was considered the foremost writer of poetry active in this country until the surging Modernist movement made his ornate kind of poetry no longer stylish. His work is still anthologized.

The Entertainers

The radio was the voice of the Depression years. It was free. It brought the world into the home: comedy, drama, commercials, the news (Lowell Thomas, Paul Sullivan at 10 o'clock from Cincinnati), music (the Metropolitan Opera on Saturday afternoons, the Philharmonic on Sundays, right here in Wilson County, as well as Paul Whiteman, Francis Craig, and Gene Austin). But the barn dance was there too, every Saturday night on WSM.

If accepted tradition and special interests and a certain bias had not acted over the years to diminish the particular role of Wilson County musicians in the Grand Ole Opry's early years, or if country music had remained a quaint little sideshow off Tin Pan Alley, James Donald Thompson, Sidney Johnson Harkreader, and Jack Jackson might not even be footnotes in the history of the county. As pioneers in what has become the great popular music movement of the twentieth century's closing decades they are important and it is important that their stories be told.

In a sense, Sid was probably the first full-time musician on the Opry. Others had regular work of other kinds but the fiddle was his life. It is documented that he was not only there when George D. Hay named the country music broadcast the "Grand Ole Opry" but had played the first tune on the show after Dr. Walter Damrosch's program of classical music on NBC had ended and the air was given back to the local station. It is also documented that he, Uncle Dave Macon, and Dr. Humphrey Bate and his Hawaiian orchestra played on the first remote control broadcast from WSM. This was no hole-in-the-wall personal appearance, but a performance before 6000 people sponsored by the Nashville Policemen's Benefit Association and held in what has come to be called "the mother church of country music," Ryman Auditorium. It occurred November 6, 1925, was advertised as "An Evening With WSM," featuring "these artists and musicians in person that you listen to over your radio every evening." The advertising in *The Tennessean* urged: "Hear Uncle Dave and Sid on the banjo and guitar."

Fiddlin' Sid and Uncle Dave had recorded for Aeolian Vocalion Record Company in New York City on July 10, 1924, and discographers say that it is almost certain they were the first from Tennessee to record traditional country music. In July 1962, Fiddlin' Sid put his first new records on the market since 1928, but collectors know those early recordings for Paramount very well.

Fiddling Sid Harkreader of
Gladeville, performer on the
first Grand Ole Opry radio
broadcast, is pictured in a
drawing by Michael Birdwell
from a contemporary poster.

Born on a farm near Gladeville February 26, 1898, in a log
cabin which burned while he was an infant, Harkreader grew
up on the farm, plowing corn, cuting wood, and milking cows.
His first fiddle was made by his father from a cornstalk and broom
wire. He moved to a Hohner harmonica bought at Lohman's store,
and then when he was 15 to a real fiddle bought from Sears Roe-
buck with $3.95 he earned trapping. The fiddle is on display in
Roy Acuff's museum. Fiddlers' contests, school shows with Uncle
Dave, and theater engagements led eventually to WSM.

Uncle Jimmy Thompson was 77 years old on November 28,
1925, when George D. Hay asked him to play on the radio. Within
a month he was known all over the country. If the Police Benefit
is considered a special event, then that more or less impromptu
show from the studio was the beginning of regular country music programming on WSM. The first tune Uncle Jimmy played
on his fiddle was "Tennessee Wagoner," as best anyone can remember. After an hour, according to the best known anecdote,
Hay suggested the old man might be tired, evoking the reply:
"An hour? Fiddlesticks! A man can't get warmed up in an hour.
I just won an eight-day fiddling contest down in Dallas and here's
my blue ribbon to prove it. This program's got to be longer."

The best evidence is that the name "Grand Ole Opry" was
given in January 1926, although it did not appear in radio programs until December 1927. Handbills used the name earlier

than this. At any rate Uncle Jimmy was not playing regularly after mid-1927 and historian Charles K. Wolfe, whose 1975 book *The Grand Ole Opry: The Early Years, 1925–1935* is by far the most dependable source, says Uncle Jimmy appeared on the Opry only once in 1928. He still made records, although the record business was slipping fast, but on February 17, 1931, he died of pneumonia. There are five different versions of the cause, but all agree it was basically exposure to freezing weather. Not until June 1975 was his grave marked with funds given by WSM, the Opry, and country music fans and musicians.

Uncle Jimmy was born James Donald Thompson near Baxter. The family moved to Texas. He was too young for the Civil War but learned fiddle tunes from returning soldiers. He returned to Smith County to farm, then went back to Texas where he started performing in public with the fiddle. It was in 1907 that he won the blue ribbon in Dallas. His style, Wolfe thinks, was the "Texas long bow," more elaborate than that of Tennessee fiddlers. He came back to Tennessee in 1912, married a LaGuardo girl, Ella Manners, as his second wife, and lived there the rest of his life. His niece, Eva Thompson Jones, a teacher of music and dancing, was responsible for bringing the old man and George Hay together when she invited the program manager to her house the evening of November 27, 1925, to hear her uncle play. The rest is on the record.

But Lebanon and Wilson County also remember another performance: Uncle Jimmy captured their hearts when he competed against former Governor Bob Taylor and won the big fiddling contest against "Our Bob" and 42 other fiddlers with a spirited rendition of "Dixie.'

Jack Jackson is a welder by vocation. He used to advertise "We weld everything but the break of day." He loves to experiment. He has made a music stand, a dictionary stand, a couch vibrator with cushions that vibrate individually, and once welded a pair of gold spectacle frames. But many of his friends and neighbors do not know him as "The Strolling Yodeler" nor do they know that he made the very first recording ever made in Nashville in 1928. (He says "about 1927 or 1928" but Wolfe documents the event as "1928, when Victor held the first recording session in Nashville.")

Jackson recalls that, in January 1926, some friends got a spot on WLAC in Nashville and "hunted me up to make a noise with them." They appeared once a month for 15 minutes of air time. One day an extra quarter hour opened up unexpectedly and Jackson was asked to fill in. He picked on his guitar for 15 extra minutes and not long after was booked for a regular weekly show which later expanded to two or three times a week. He played quite a few dates with Sid Harkreader and was responsible for Harkreader entering a contest at Hopkinsville, Kentucky, where Sid won a trip to the 1933 World's Fair in Chicago. Apparently Jackson, who was born between Leeville and Gladeville and began his radio career when 17, never sang on the Opry proper unless as vocalist for the Binkley Brothers' Dixie Clodhoppers. However, in the 1930s published WSM programs do occasionally contain the listing, "Jack Jackson," indicating that he may have had his own show for a while. WSM never lists him by his better known professional name, "The Strolling Yodeler." Other Wilson countians who appeared on early programs were Julius Robinson, Bill and Sam Rucker, L. H. Ingram, and Lewis Crook. The Ruckers and Robinson called themselves the Gladeville Trio. Crook is one of the Crook Brothers but he and Herman Crook are not brothers, not kin at all.

Lebanon's most recent Opry connection was Ralph Sloan, leader of the square dance group, the Tennessee Travelers (regulars for 11 years on the syndicated television show "That Nashville Music"), and an Opry member from 1952 until his death in 1980. He first became interested in country music when he was given a ukulele for Christmas when he was five. Sloan once told this writer that he had walked two miles to the home of a neighbor who owned a radio just so he could hear Roy Acuff and Ernest Tubb. Square dances were a regular weekend event at Cedars of Lebanon state park after 1939 and Sloan was employed as a doorman. It was then he learned to square dance.

The Flatt & Scruggs team of country musicians was discovered by Efford Burke of Lebanon in 1953 when they were playing over Station WNOX, Knoxville. Burke, a salesman for Martha White Mills, introduced them to Cohen T. Williams, head of the company. Martha White sponsored the team on WSM and the Opry for 20 years.

Many Wilson countians have been associated with popular music, more than can be named. Jack Pursley played flute and clarinet in the Sousa band. Songwriter John Loudermilk was born between Gladeville and Mt. Juliet. Elmo Tanner of Mt. Juliet was with the Ted Weems orchestra, his best known recording having been "Heartaches" which featured Tanner's whistling. Owen Bradley located the first recording studio, "Bradley's Barn," famous among popular musicians, near Green Hill. Floyd & Baxter Amusement Company, formed by Dallas, J.D., and Jimmy Floyd and Billy Baxter of Lebanon, has played major fairs across the United States and Canada and has had some units in Hawaii. Their wives, Inza, Ann, and Janet Floyd and Jane Floyd Baxter, made the road trips with them, traveling in two tractor-trailer rigs converted into rolling homes.

The Cedars of Lebanon

An enduring result of the Depression years is Cedars of Lebanon park and state forest. Eight miles south of Lebanon on Highway 231 is dense woodland, the largest remaining forest of red cedar (more properly, Virginia juniper) in the country. In 1933 the Resettlement Administration of the U.S. Department of Ariculture chose this site, at the suggestion of a nearby landowner and former Department of Agriculture official, Dixon Merritt, as a submarginal land project, reforestation program, and recreational area. It was proposed that with a long period of reforestation revenue could be realized from the production and sale of cedar and employment could be provided through the Works Progress Administration for the jobless.

The cedars of Lebanon of Biblical times played an important role in the building of the Temple of King Solomon. In Wilson County the soil in certain sections is especially suited for producing the red cedar. In the area near Hunter's Point trees of large dimension were growing on the Chapman farm. In older houses and barns exceptionally large cedar logs were found. A pencil mill in operation on the southern border of Lebanon had been processing pencil slats of cedar wood for many years and was making extensive shipments of cedar for lining closets. Zig-zag rail fences were a familiar sight, until the demand for cedar wood led to their demolition and sale. Even large cedar poles and beams were taken from feed barns and sold for needed cash, to be shipped to the Southwest where the demand for cedar fence posts seemed insatiable. Larger trees went to furniture makers who produced chests of solid cedar. By 1930 almost all saleable cedar had been cut and sold, leaving only the very poor subsoil, of no value for agriculture. In the section near Baird's Mill and Vine this was particularly true.

The Agriculture Adjustment Agency was already in operation, under the local direction of County Agent Louis Sawyer. Under the name of Wilson County Cedar Forest project, later the Lebanon Cedar Forest, initial work was approved with the stipulation that the land would be acquired from owners by tracts and a large area "blocked." An office was opened in the Coaplen Building on the Lebanon Public Square, adjacent to the AAA headquarters. The first personnel appointments were: project manager, Merrill Wise, soon to be replaced by E. S. Permenter; surveyor-engineer, John E. Perry, a former state senator who had helped establish the Great Smoky Mountains National Park; secretary underclerk, Ruby Foutch (now Mrs. William Vann); option clerk, Guthrie Sullivan. Landowners were located and options signed for the most barren land at $2 to $26 per acre, averaging $6 for the area of some 9000 acres. "Miss Ruby" searched the courthouse records, locating the survey calls for "Squire" Perry who then "tied" the tracts on the project map. If there were only boundary calls, the tracts were actually surveyed. It was a tedious task and until still more owners were signed purchase and development approval was not given. After approval, development appointments were made: Arthur Jurgens as field engineer; Michael E. Jelley, forester; Edward Kirkpatrick, office manager; Gladys Ferrell, payroll clerk; Albert Bryan, surveyor; D. P. Coffee, carpenter and cabinet maker; W. Collier Parrish, project engineer; E. P. Butler, Henry Harrell, and Buford Keene, draftsmen; Lon P. MacFarland and O. W. McKensie, legal staff; and George T. Nelson, construction superintendent. Working as chain boys were Charles Howard Baird, Hollis Edwards, Lindsey B. Hopkins, and Ben Huddleston; Katie Lee Drennan, Lillie Hodge, and Blanche Ligon were office assistants. The staff outgrew its quarters and moved to a dwelling house on University Avenue, Lebanon. From 1934 to 1939 the work proceeded.

Plans were drafted and bids taken, locally where possible. Local residents were employed as foremen and at the peak of development some hundred WPA workers were on the payroll. A once-abandoned area was turned into a working unit. Native cedar, stone, and other materials created a blend of old and new. The lodge of stone and cedar trim had an open fireplace with an old millstone from a nearby farm mounted above the mantel. Cabins were furnished with handmade furniture. Along the 1½-mile asphalt drive from the masonry and rock entrance was a zigzag rail fence behind which grew native redbud trees. Adjacent to the lodge was an Olympic-sized pool and bath house, picnic areas, a wading pool for children, and a snack bar. Inside the lodge were a dance hall for square dancing, a sun porch, party and game rooms, and two massive fireplaces.

To restore the cedar trees a nursery was instituted where the most unexpected problem was finally ingeniously solved by Forester Jelley and his workers. Cedar berry seed would not germinate at first. In nature the berries are planted by birds. Finally it was suspected that the scratching action of the bird's bill on the berry was essential, as well as the temperature of winter soil on which the dormant berry had to lie for a season. Cedar trees were shaken over sheets of cloth, berries gathered and frozen in ice at the Interstate Ice & Coal Company for several weeks, and then scarified, prompting germination. The process produced great numbers of seedlings in plant boxes which were successfully transplanted. Meanwhile bushels of walnuts were gathered and planted in rows. Native trees of other kinds and ornamentals were set out, although the extensive redbud and dogwood growth that makes the trails and roads spectacular in the spring is natural.

After the lodge was completed but not yet ready for public use, office personnel moved from University Avenue. Some employees were permitted to rent the finished cabins, the project administrators being conscious of saving government money. In fact, the women employees would bring prepared vegetables and foods, the men money, and by midday the food was ready for a small family hot lunch. Occasionally a visiting official would be invited to dine, if caught "out in the country" at mealtime, and his "tip" would be appreciated. It was a happy crew. But this could not last for long. Once the lodge was ready for public use the office was moved to a cabin, workers left as their jobs were finished, and Gladys Ferrell was the last to close the door in 1939.

In that year the area was leased to the Tennessee Department of Conservation as Cedars of Lebanon State Park. The federal government deeded it to the state in 1955. It is now classified as a day-use park and contains 8887 acres, 901 of them used for intensive recreation. The remainder is operated by the Division of Parks as a natural area and by the Division of Forestry as a state forest, the largest forest of red cedar remaining in the United States. It is a remarkable natural area where 19 rare wild flowers may be found in and around the cedar glades. In the spring the poor and barren soil awakens with color which varies from week to week throughout the season. The uninitiated may see this plant growth as plentiful and unimportant but the botanist appreciates its rarity; many of the plants are found only in a few counties of Tennessee and Alabama. About half of the species were so rare that they could not be found in reference books.

In 1977 a 1043-acre section of the state forest which had been threatened by urbanization was designated a National Natural Landmark by the U.S. Department of the Interior. In 1978 the Dixon Lanier Merritt Nature Center at the lodge was dedicated. Here the story of the cedars and other plants, the animals, geology, and cultural history are interpreted.

The area is dotted with Indian mounds and numerous caves. Jackson's Cave, a quarter of a mile long, contains an underground stream with a flow of 200 gallons of water a minute in dry weather. Beyond the stream, tradition says, the bandit John Murrell hid some of the gold which he stole from travelers on the old Natchez Trace. Hermit Cave was the dwelling of Ben Coy, who grew old and died there. Goat Skull Pit is five feet in diameter and 30 feet deep. At the bottom is a small room containing a well-preserved goat skull.

The Second World War and Wilson County

During the years before Germany invaded Poland, Wilson countians were aware of increasing international tensions and many knew that when war came the United States could not long remain neutral. The Munich crisis of 1938 brought the voice of Adolf Hitler into American living rooms; newspaper headlines had brought Ethiopia and Spain closer. The Lebanon Rotary Club heard Dr. Gus Dyer of Vanderbilt discuss foreign policy; *The Lebanon Democrat* solicited a regular column on international relations from Dean Will D. Young of Cumberland. The Red Cross chapter in 1940 conducted a campaign for relief for Belgium and Holland. Italy's invasion of France was announced at the Cumberland graduation exercises in June of that year. Reserve officers were called to active duty in October, and on December 7, 1940, Lovell Rousseau was Wilson's County's first Selective Service inductee into the Army. One year later to the day radios announced that Pearl Harbor had been bombed. Rousseau returned to his home after four years, eight months, and 27 days of active duty. Wilson countians served all over the world in all branches of the Armed Forces. The Army itself came to Wilson County in 1942 for extensive training maneuvers. One million soldiers were prepared for the invasion and reconquest of Europe along the Cumberland River during the following two years.

Somewhere in Tennessee

In 1862 General John Hunt Morgan fought a pitched battle in downtown Lebanon against Federal cavalry, and some of his men stood a brief siege in the Odd Fellows hall that then stood

In 1931 the Italian government, at the invitation of Bernarr Macfadden who owned Castle Heights Military Academy, sent a group of cadets to his school for classes in physical culture. Among other social events, they were guests of the Rotary Club at dinner and a reception.

on the site occupied in 1979 by the Capitol Theatre. Morgan, a flamboyant, flashily-dressed cavalry commander with ways more colorful than any other Confederate general except possibly Jeb Stuart, did not survive his war. Neither did flamboyant, flashily-dressed tank commander George S. Patton, who led his Second Armored Division tanks down Main Street and around the West Side Hotel corner on a June night in 1941.

Patton probably did not know that his tanks were burning rubber over the same ground where Morgan had fought. Although he might have known that his maternal ancestors had moved West from Wilson County he certainly could not have suspected that he was passing the place where a motion picture about his life would be shown 29 years later. But Patton, whose grandfather was a member of the faculty of the Virginia Military Institute where so many Confederate officers had been trained, might well have admired Morgan and he certainly patterned his tank tactics after the cavalry tactics of Nathan Bedford Forrest, as did Field Marshal Erwin Rommel of the German Army. Forrest had also led his troops up that same main street of Lebanon, as had Joe Wheeler, a third great Rebel cavalry commander.

Patton told his army, after their victorious advance to Bastogne in January 1945, "The speed and brilliancy of your achievements are unsurpassed in military history." The preparation for that speed and brilliancy had been made in Middle Tennessee many months before.

Patton ended the war in command of the largest army in American history. There were 500,000 men in the Third Army as it moved across Czechoslovakia. On June 17, 1941, he was in command of one armored division, and there were only two of them in the entire American army. Patton's Second "Hell on Wheels" Division contained 11,000 men and 2300 vehicles. That June morning when it attacked a "Blue" infantry division southeast of Murfreesboro was the first time in American military annals that a full armored division had engaged in maneuvers or had an opportunity to test itself in combat.

It was shortly after midnight that the residents of East Main Street were roused from sleep by the thunder, creaking, and roaring of machines. A flying squadron of motorcycles was the first to pound down East Main, across the Public Square, and, rounding the West Side Hotel corner, race out South Maple Street toward Murfreesboro on old State Highway 10 (South Cumberland Street, later to become U.S. Highway 231, in 1941 ended near the old depot). Armored combat cars equipped with machine guns and radio followed the motorcycles and then came the light tanks, burning dim blue "blackout" lights and protruding 37mm cannon from buttoned-up turrets.

For hour after hour the armored might of Patton, who had been in the leading command element, rolled through Lebanon. Each tank carried a crew of four: driver, assistant driver, gunner, and radio operator. Besides the cannon the tanks were armed with .30 and .50 caliber machine guns. The convoy moved out the Murfreesboro Pike at 60 miles an hour. After the tanks came jeeps, six-by-six personnel carriers, ambulances, and supply trucks—an entire division on the move, complete with supporting engineer units with pontoon bridges, water purification equipment, earth augers, and signal units.

This was only the beginning of Lebanon's role in World War

The Second Army maneuvers of 1942–1944 brought nearly a million soldiers into Wilson County preparing for the conquest of Europe. Here a medic and an infantryman wait for an umpire vehicle to pass through the lines near Doak's Cross Roads.

II. These were light tanks. The bigger, heavier Shermans were to become even more familiar. Instead of 37mm cannon, the Murfreesboro Pike was soon to tremble under the weight of the 105mm "Long Toms." Instead of one division, there were to be as many as five operating within the county at one time. In all, 28 divisions and many detached units and corps were trained in the Tennessee Maneuver Area, with Second Army Maneuver Director Headquarters at Cumberland University. The 101st Airborne Division conducted the first airborne landing under battle conditions near Taylorsville in 1943, a rehearsal for the D-Day airborne landing in Normandy a year later. The Cumberland River was a stand-in for the Rhine, Stone's River for the Ruhr. Middle Tennesseans became more familiar with the realities of war than any other Americans not in the Armed Forces, with the exception of those who were living in the Louisiana Maneuver Area of the Third Army.

The Sixth of June

They called it D-Day, there in the buildings in Grosvenor Square, as they moved blue squares on the great war map. Blue squares, cardboard, thumbtacks, moved slowly, so slowly, down a map of Normandy. And there on the beach called Omaha, how slowly moved the men beneath the German steel.

In the war room was a man from Lebanon, Col. Tom Crawford. On the beach were men who wore the Blue and Gray again. The blue and gray? Yes; on the shoulders of the 29th Infantry Division was the blue and gray patch that represented the once divided loyalties of Maryland, the state to whose National Guard the division had once belonged, the unity of once divided states. Once more federalized as they had been in 1918, the Guardsmen (originally from New Jersey and Delaware, Maryland and Virginia, and the District of Columbia) landed on the battered beach called Omaha. But what has the 29th with its blue and gray shoulder patch to do with Wilson County, Tennessee?

Its general was born on Hatton Avenue, Lebanon, and reared in a house on East Spring Street built by his father, teacher of military science and tactics at Cumberland University from 1894 to 1897. Charles Gerhardt was the only Wilson County soldier to hold the rank of major general in World War II. June 6 was more than D-Day to Charles Hunter Gerhardt. It was his 49th birthday.

He went ashore with his troops, inched up the cliffs and the high bluff with them, and spent the night of D-Day in a rock quarry just 300 yards from the beach. It was the luck of the 29th to draw the sector where the German army had concentrated its heaviest defenses. One company lost all of its officers but one before its assault boats ever landed on the beach. Within minutes after another company touched the beach, it was out of action, every man killed or wounded, huddled weaponless against the base of the cliff. But it was not to be a day of defeat. Slowly the men edged off Omaha Beach. By the end of the day the 29th was a mile inland. Omaha Beach was followed by Isigny. There General Gerhardt moved among his troops as they advanced on the outskirts of the town, disregarding land mines, rifle bullets, and machine gun fire.

It earned him a Silver Star. Isigny led to St. Lô, and St. Lô to Brittany, and then to the Rhine and peace on the Elbe.

There were other Silver Stars brought home to Wilson County from that day in Normandy. First to land were airborne soldiers of the 101st, the division whose first landing in training had occurred a year before near Taylorsville in Wilson County. Leonard Beard earned his Silver Star with the 101st on D-Day. Willie Webster did too. Sergeant Beard, who landed with a glider regiment, was personally decorated by General Dwight D. Eisenhower.

The GIs

At Corregidor Pvt. Andrew Oscar Woodall and Pfc. Robert E. Barnett were members of the antiaircraft battalion that brought down two enemy bombers in one day. At Guadalcanal Pfc. John B. Maddux made the landing with the Marines in August 1942 and stayed until hospitalized with malaria, holding on under fierce shelling and enemy bombardment. With the Fifth Army in Italy as Headquarters Battery, IV Corps Artillery, and in the South Pacific and the Philippines as Headquarters Battery, XI Corps Artillery, the National Guardsmen from Wilson County, divided before going overseas, fought two of the most difficult campaigns of the war. In the Huertgen Forest with the Fourth Infantry Division in November 1944 Pvt. Herman Eskew Jr. trudged soaked through pines dripping with cold rain. In December, Staff Sgt. James E. Knowles, T/5 Joseph J. Chenault, and T/5 William Andrew Belcher found their regiment of the 106th Infantry Division blasted by the avalanche of enemy steel and fire that was the Battle of the Bulge. Chenault and Belcher were captured, Knowles died of wounds. Early in 1945 at Remagen, trying to keep the bridge across the Rhine open, T/4 Donald Smotherman and his engineer battalion went down with the bridge when it finally collapsed. At Mukden, Manchuria, in August Major Ernest L. Brown, Wilson County's most decorated serviceman of the war, captured on Bataan in 1942, was released from prison camp by Soviet troops.

The telegrams began arriving at the Western Union office in

the West Side Hotel in February, 1942. Before the end of August, 1945, there had been more than 80. The dead were:

Wilburn Adams, Bernice Ash, Charles Crawford Barbour, Joe Frank Barton, Charles William Bass, William L. Bridges, James Otha Bryan, William W. Burkett, Charles Lee Burton, Joe Raymond Carter, Edward Christian, Henry Murray Comer, Ray Conatser, George L. Davis, Talmadge E. Davis, James Alford Dockins, Robert T. Donnell, Meredith Eugene Draper, William G. Dunnaway, Blanton B. Dye.

Robert L. Forrester, Jr., Howard Owen Garrett, Bryan Rhea Gilliam, Walter Turner Hankins, Jr., Lawrence Hamlet, Glenn C. Haralson, Roydon E. Hardaway, George Holdsworth, John Harvey Holland, Will Ben Holland, Ponie Lea Jenkins, William Franklin Jenkins, Willie L. Jones, David D. Kelley, Robert N. King, William Knight (first from Wilson County), James E. Knowles, James L. Lackey, Herbert B. Lawson, Robert Lawson.

Walter Fisher Martin, William J. Mitchell, Judson Mofield, Robert L. Moody, James H. Murphy, Jr., Melton C. Nettles, J. C. Odum, Joe Palmer, John M. "Red" Palmer, Carwin Oakley Parker, Clarence Peak, Roy Wendell Phillips, Nathan Wesley Pope, William C. Ragland, Fred Reeder, Oscar E. Reynolds, Phillip Rice, James T. "Roxie" Rice, Hardin W. Robertson, Jr., John Fite Robertson, Jr., Robert L. Rodgers.

James Clyde Seale, Charlie Lofton Sherrill, Edwin Winfield "Buck" Smith, James Howard Smith, William V. Smithson, Donald Smotherman, Joe W. Speck, George L. Sullivan, Harry Summers, Harry Swann (first from Lebanon), Riley C. Thompson, Edward Glenn Walker, Henry Dean Waters, Clarence F. Webb, Thomas E. White, Horace Vale Williams, Brownie Witt, Joe E. Wright, William Edsel Wright, and William Clyde York.

Hateful Little Wars

Everyone knows about December 7 and November 11. Some can identify April 19, 1775. But who can name the day the Vietnam War began? Or ended? What is Armistice Day for veterans of Korea?

On June 27, 1950, armed forces of North Korea crossed the 38th parallel of latitude, dividing line between the occupation zones set up by the Allies after Japan surrendered. Within a month a Wilson County soldier had been captured; within another three weeks a Lebanon soldier had been killed. Robert Stanley, Jr., was a member of the 21st Infantry Regiment, 24th Division, and was in the first planeload of United States troops to land in Korea on June 30, 1950. A World War II veteran who had reenlisted, he was captured July 5 during the great retreat into the Pusan perimeter and spent 37 months as a prisoner of war in Chiang-Song Camp. (Stanley died December 13, 1979, at the age of 51.) At Waegwon on August 7 Pvt. Paul Haynes was killed in action with the 5th Cavalry regiment, and as the conflict continued seven more servicemen from Wilson County gave their lives: Clarence L. Farmer, Odis M. Harris, Joseph Rhea Pursley, Johnnie E. Rhodes, Charles E. Rodgers, Calvin Coolidge Vick, Claude Mason Williams. Many Wilson countians won high awards. The Distinguished Service Cross went to Sgt. Claude Walls for extraordinary heroism in action with the Second Infantry Division in stopping the Chinese offensive. (In World War I the decoration, second only to the Medal of Honor, had been earned by Lt. Avis T. Hobbs; in World War II, by Maj. Ernest L. Brown.) Sfc. William Cartmell and Staff Sgt. Miller W. Scott received the Silver Star. Lt. Col. Edwin W. Richardson received the Legion of Merit. On July 27, 1953, an armistice between the North Koreans and the United Nations forces was signed at Panmunjom. A demilitarized zone still separates the two armies after nearly 30 years.

Less than 10 years later, in 1961, American military advisers went into Vietnam; helicopter pilots in 1962. The U.S. Congress adoped the Gulf of Tonkin Resolution in 1964 and Marines were sent to Da Nang. Thus America slid almost imperceptibly into a state of war. On December 17, 1964, *The Lebanon Democrat* in an editorial by Frank Burns entitled "Give More Light" stated: "Without vision, the people perish, says the text. The people perish even faster without enlightenment. The American public is not adequately informed about Vietnam." The editorial, which went on to demand authoritative answers, was the first published in any newspaper in the South to question the American role in Asia. By 1970 there were eight Wilson countians dead.

Joseph D. Bailey was the first. A sergeant first class with the 5th Special Forces, he was sent to Camp Plei-Me in April 1965. He had already received the Combat Infantryman's badge and the Vietnam parachute badge. The Arkansas native turned down an appointment to West Point to enlist in the Army paratroops and served in Germany. While stationed at Fort Campbell he met and married Alice Rachel Chastain of Lebanon. He joined the Special Forces in order to be assigned to Vietnam. On Wednesday, October 20, he was killed as 500 Viet Cong surrounded Plei-Me and hit the camp with mortar and machine gun fire. Bailey had raised a small American flag beside the gold and red ARVN standard and told Associated Press photographer Eddie Adams: "If we've got to go down, we'll go down under our own colors." The photograph appeared in newspapers all over the United States.

There followed the deaths of seven more Wilson countians including James Edward Bush and Billy Edward Stevenson in 1966; Jerry David Lancaster and Clyde Anderson Ward in 1967; Terry Lee Dillard and Ronnie C. Presley in 1968; and John Thomas Burton in 1969. Maj. William Burkart's plane vanished in flight over Hanoi and he was listed as missing in action as the war dragged on.

Lancaster, who was a Specialist 4th with the 28th Infantry regiment, First Division, when he was killed on October 17, 1967, had commenced his tour in Vietnam March 10 of that year. At this time the heaviest fighting was in the northernmost provinces of South Vietnam and assumed the characteristics of the war in Korea: armies facing each other on a defined front. Lancaster was reported dead "as the result of a gunshot wound received in hostile ground action 17 October, 1967." It was in fact a last frontal assault by a foe preparing to send the war into a new phase, the Tet offensive. Tet was a military defeat for the North; but it was a disastrous psychological and propaganda defeat for the United States.

Another Specialist 4th class, John Richard Fessler, who survived, summarized his experiences in a letter to his parents, Mr. and Mrs. Robert Fessler. It may anticipate the eventual judgment of history. Fessler wrote in August 1968: "Some of the things about Viet-Nam only I will ever know. This land is plagued with a dirty, miserable war that seems to be never ending. Every time you see a small child, or any one of the Vietnamese, you can see the thanks in their eyes for the job us guys are over here to do. They only want to be left alone so that they may live in peace. Lots of times at night I go down to the gate at the entrance to the compound and watch the families come in from the field. It is so very pitiful. The little kids of 4 and 5 years old put in their day of work just as the grown-ups do. You can hear them chatter in the distance as they walk up the road to their houses and then you hear the sounds of war."

In January 1973 direct American military involvement on the ground in Asia ended. On April 30, 1975, the army of North Vietnam marched victoriously into Saigon.

Commanders With Three Stars

Because it is very seldom indeed that a single nonmetropolitan county is home for one, much less two three-star (lieutenant) generals at once, the award of a third star to two Wilson County general officers in a single year should be put on the record.

The year was 1978. The officers were Carl Wallace and Eugene Forrester. The first was the Adjutant General of Tennessee, an office which customarily carries the rank of major general and two stars. General Wallace was the first adjutant general of the state to attain the rank of lieutenant general; he took office under Governor Ray Blanton, who recommended the promotion, and continued under Governor Lamar Alexander. When promoted he was 47, and had been editor of *The Lebanon Democrat* since 1964. He received his commission in 1951, served on active duty during the Korean Conflict, and remained in the National Guard after resuming his newspaper career in 1953.

General Forrester, a native of Watertown, was promoted to the rank of lieutenant general and named commanding general of the Sixth Army with headquarters at the Presidio of San Francisco. The appointment and promotion of General Forrester from the rank of major general was announced by Secretary of Defense Harold Brown. In November 1979 he was named to command the First Corps, Republic of Korea–United States Group—over 180,000 soldiers occupying a series of defensive positions along the Demilitarized Zone which separates North and South Korea. General Forrester was 52 when he received the third star and had graduated from the U.S. Military Academy in 1948. He had attended the public schools of Watertown and graduated from Watertown High School in 1944. He served with commands in Austria, England, France, the Dominican Republic, Korea and Vietnam as well as in various assignments within the United States.

Although other Wilson County officers had worn two stars, only one other had the official rank of lieutenant general. He was Alexander P. Stewart, a West Pointer like Forrester, who rose from command of a battery to command the remnants of the Army of Tennessee. The third star was granted Stewart in June of 1864, when he was assigned command of the corps formerly under Leonidas Polk. Born in 1821, he came to Cumberland University in 1845 as professor of mathematics. He built the residence on East Spring Street now occupied by Dr. and Mrs. Sam McFarland. Coincidentally, a house diagonally across the street was the childhood home of a two-star general of World War II, Charles Hunter Gerhardt, commander of the 29th Infantry Division which landed in Normandy on D-Day.

Five other general officers have called Wilson County their home. Robert Hopkins Hatton, brigadier general of the Army of Virginia, and a former United States Congressman, was killed at Seven Pines on May 31, 1862. Harry Thompson Hays, was first commander of the 7th Louisiana Infantry and then brigadier in the Army of Northern Virginia; he served at Sharpsburg, Chancellorsville, Gettysburg, the Wilderness, and other major battles. John Selden Roane, former governor of Arkansas, was commissioned brigadier in March 1862. Jesse Finley, veteran of the Seminole War and former mayor of Memphis, commanded the Florida regiments after November 1863 and subsequently became a United States Congressman. William Bowen Campbell, former governor of Tennessee, United States Congressman (1838-1844, 1865-1867), and colonel commanding the First Tennessee Regiment of Volunteers at the Battle of Monterrey in the war with Mexico, was commissioned a brigadier general in 1861 by President Lincoln. His signed commisson hangs in the head-quarters of Fort Campbell, Kentucky, which was named for him in 1942.

Postwar Developments in Commerce and Industry

The immediate postwar decade in Wilson County was a time of stagnation, out-migration, and readjustment. A new city administration took office in January 1949 whose priorities were to modernize utilities and public facilities that had deteriorated during the depression and war years and to improve public recreation opportunities. Lebanon had known much progress from 1936 to 1941 but its returning economic health had depended mostly on large enrollments in the law school. The Army's presence from 1942 to 1944 had pumped much cash into the local economy, but roads and streets, electric, water, and gas systems, commercial buildings, and industrial plants had steadily deteriorated.

A Decade of Industrial Development

In the 1960s Lebanon and Wilson County were featured in the national press, not once but several times, and each of these events that attracted nationwide attention were representative of economic and social trends.

The Ross Gear story, which appeared in both *Time* and *U.S. News & World Report*, concerned the lawsuit that determined the right of a company to choose a new location for its factory. In *Newsweek* appeared the story of the removal of Cumberland School of Law to Birmingham, an action that saved both the law school and the liberal arts college but subtly changed the cultural and social character of the town. An article in *National Business Woman* discussed Lebanon's approach to the school dropout problem.

Dr. Frank Baddour *(left)* receives a community service award from Howard K. Edgerton, president of the Lebanon Woolen Mills. Dr. Baddour was vice-mayor of Lebanon.

There was an article in *The Tennessee Planner* which presented Lebanon's development of an industrial subdivision as a model plan. And "The Lebanon Story," U.S. Children's Bureau publication No. 395–1961, told how this community was able to adapt findings of the White House Conference on Children and Youth, to which Dr. Billy M. Hightower of Lebanon was a delegate.

Most of these stories had their true beginning on a July day in 1952 when a telegram arrived from the Firestone Tire & Rubber Company, calling off plans to build a large plant in Lebanon. That day was probably the darkest in Mayor William Donnell Baird's life. But the disappointment inspired such efforts in subsequent months that, instead of one new industry, by 1969 (the years of its sesquicentennial celebration) Lebanon had a dozen or more diversified factories providing 5300 adult jobs. As mayor and later as chairman of the Tennessee Agricultural and Industrial Development Commission, Baird devoted unlimited personal time and money, without reimbursement, to the cause of industrialization as a key to slowing the out-migration of young people, a human resource that could not be squandered by a community hoping to remain economically and socially healthy. "Every one of you has money in your pocket as the result of work Bill Baird did at his own expense for your state," Governor Frank Clement once told a group of Tennesseans.

In 1950 Lebanon had only three plants that employed as many as 100 persons; Watertown had one; Mt. Juliet, a suburban residential community, none. The annual industrial payroll 25 years later exceeded $30 million. That figure was above Bill Baird's fondest dreams when he first advocated the development of Lebanon's municipal industrial subdivision of 278 acres. He patterned it on similar areas in Atlanta and other large areas of the South, but Lebanon was the first municipality in Tennessee to develop such a tract, fully served by city streets, utilities, and railroad spur tracks.

The first new industries to acquire land in the subdivision were Lebanon Manufacturing Company (now Precision Rubber) and Hartmann Luggage Company, the former based in Dayton, Ohio, the second in Racine, Wisconsin. Hartmann moved its main offices to Lebanon and used this address in its extensive advertising campaign for its prestige products. It is now one of the five largest luggage manufacturers in the United States. Soon afterward came Ross Gear & Tool (originally Gemmer when located in Detroit, now called TRW-Ross Gear division). The parade had started.

Bill Baird got his training in industrial development the hard way, with Firestone executives as the teachers. The mayor took office in January 1949, following the retirement of Frank Buchanan; that year Hearne Partee established the Partee Boat Company, and Harry Vise the Texas Boot Manufacturing Company in 1951. But it was the long exhausting negotiations with the tire company, the mayor, and other interested citizens that taught

In January 1960 William D. Baird *(center, seated)* took office as mayor of Lebanon for the last time. He resigned in June to devote more time to the office of lieutenant governor. That administration included *(from left, seated)* Aldermen J. C. Johnson, Harry Beard, Charles Loyd (who succeeded to the mayoralty), Joe Graves; *(standing)* Commissioner of Public Works Gene Weatherby, Attorney Sam Gilreath, Chief of Police and Fire Dallas Young, Assistant Chief Maurice Young, Building Inspector George Hodges, Tax Assessor, O. F. Williams, Back Tax Attorney Daniel Seay, Commissioner of Finance Bob McConnell, Planning Commission Chairman George Harding.

the big lessons. Land was acquired. Contacts were made. Labor was registered. Yale & Towne had been interested in the same site for a lock plant but, because Lebanon officials thought Firestone was sewn up, told to go elsewhere. Then Firestone, involved in complicated union negotiations at its Virginia plant, decided not to move at that time. A Connecticut clock manufacturer, Fred Lux, became interested in Tennessee as a location for a new branch plant. It was to make spring-driven alarm clocks, which the company sold principally in the Southeast. Bill Baird prepared Lebanon's case and spent days of his time in presenting it. The effort was successful. Joe Atkinson, whose wartime Navy service had been in a torpedo boat squadron with John F. Kennedy and whose college football coaching career had been spent in part with Paul F. "Bear"Bryant at the University of Kentucky, moved from the positon of head coach at Lebanon High School to manager of the Lux plant. Generally the new industries brought management personnel with them, but not always. Almost always the production employes were hired locally.

Mayor's Baird's alarm at the out-migration of young people led to his interest in industrialization. He saw in that migration a waste in human terms and a waste of the millions of dollars spent in educating young people who would spend their productive lives elsewhere. He had always been interested in education. Many gave him credit for finally saving Cumberland University for Lebanon in 1951 when it seemed that the institution would be removed to Nashville, for it was his offer of municipal sponsorship that was decisive in that crisis. Education, he knew, looks toward the future. Bill Baird knew that no community can live by the purely material alone. Here in an industrial subdivision, acres that had formerly been pasture and crop land in an agrarian economy, was the perfect opportunity to blend the two needs—retain the human resources by providing a means of material support.

Western Wilson County

Needmore, Green Hill, Mt. Juliet, Belinda City, Gladeville— each community with its own story, all blending into the larger community known as West Wilson—the story of western Wilson County has been for nearly 200 years the story of people moving east from Nashville. Even the oldest of these communities, Green Hill, came into being as the Cloyd-Williamson settlement because John Cloyd and John Williamson and their families sought safety from a smallpox epidemic that had broken out in Nashville. Col. John Donelson, Jr., located his summer home at Green Hill because he believed the rolling, fertile hills were more healthy than his residence on Stone's River.

Cotton and corn were the main crops. Where St. Paul's United

Methodist church is now located there was once a cotton gin and nearby on the present South Green Hill Road was the William-sons' saw and grist mill. The store, where justices of the peace held court in the nineteenth century, was in the front yard of the present Green Hill Baptist Church. On the present Old Hickory Lake, Harbor Island was once known as Fort Hill. Not only was there a fort from which Union soldiers kept watch on the river during the Civil War but arrowheads found there indicate it had been a stronghold much earlier.

Green Hill was quite likely named for the former state treasurer of North Carolina whose Seawell and Mabry kin lived not far away. Mt. Juliet was named for "Aunt Julie" or Julia Gleaves, near whose home the original village founded in 1835 was located on a high hill on the old Lebanon and Nashville dirt road. Here, too, was the famous Eagle Tavern, where Aaron Burr stayed while conferring secretly with Andrew Jackson as he planned this great Natchez intrigue. The old road is the western end of the "Old Holstein Trace" which cut diagonally across the county from Three Forks (Watertown) past old Center Hill and Doak's Cross Roads. The traveler from Nashville east would pass John Taitt's mill on Stoner's Creek, following a ridge, crossing the creek twice, the second time south of the present Mt. Juliet (relocated when the railroad was built north of the old site after the Civil War), and topping the rise that was the "Mount" could see less than a mile away the two-story log building. The wagon would pass the Gleaves home and turn into the yard, where hard by the tavern stood a log whiskey bar.

In the 1830s the Hermitage stage road was built, its macadamized surface attracting much of the traffic from the old road. Not until 1869, however, did the building of the Tennessee & Pacific Railroad cause the village to be moved to its present location. There in 1812 Cloyd's Cumberland Presbyterian Church had begun soon after the birth of the new religious body, but brush arbor meetings had been held at the location as early as 1795. Mt. Juliet is also the location of the oldest bank in Wilson County, established as the Bank of Mt. Juliet in 1908 and named

In 1840 George W. Martin came from North Carolina and established his candy store beside the new Hermitage Turnpike to Nashville. He also operated the first toll gate west of Lebanon. Known as "the toll gate house," the building stood until the mid-1950s. Pictured are Mr. and Mrs. Martin and their daughter Notie.

the First Southern Bank in 1981. This was the first bank in Tennessee to be examined by a state bank examiner.

In the 1940s Mt. Juliet got a chance to rise from the ashes—literally. A young pyromaniac set fire in turn, over a period of several months, to the lodge hall, elementary school, hotel, post office, several business houses, and the First Baptist Church. Once the crisis was past, the community undertook rebuilding with vigor. In 1959 the West Wilson Utility District began to construct water lines. Ten years later it served 1484 customers; 32 months after that, on November 1, 1971, the total was 2225. That was only the beginning of unprecedented growth during the next decade. Fifteen subdivisions were developed north of Highway 70, led by Langford's Cove, located on part of L. C. Langford's nationally known dairy cattle farm. After the impoundment of Percy Priest Lake residential development in southwest Wilson County moved steadily ahead. In 1972 Mt. Juliet was incorporated with an area of 5.5 square miles and a population of 2030,

In November 1959 the final connection of the Mt. Juliet water system
was installed. Ernest Sutherland makes the connection, watched by Gene
Grissim, Bob Bass, Sam Bates, Bill Hayes, and Jackie Hayes.

an industrial park, and a high school under direction of Principal Elzie Patton that is considered one of the most progressive
in the state.

    To move forward a community needs a moving force, some
person of dynamic energies constructively channeled. Such a
person was Thomas Harvey Freeman. Born at Silver Springs in
1835, he received the Bachelor of Arts degree from Cumberland
University in 1858, married Nancy Curd in 1860, enlisted as a
first lieutenant in the 45th Tennessee Infantry in 1861 and saw
service in the Battle of Shiloh. In May 1862 he returned home
and for a time farmed. Business was his natural vocation, although he had in early life taught school and served as county
superintendent of public instruction in 1877 and 1878. He traded
in land and was a banker, helping to found the Bank of Mt. Juliet

of which he was president. He financed many local enterprises, and he became the publisher of a newspaper at Mt. Juliet, *Mt. Juliet News*. As county superintendent he established the Teacher Institute that met annually for more than 30 years as professional in-service training. In 1889 he and another educator, B. M. Mace, who had followed Freeman as superintendent, were sent to the General Assembly as direct representatives (the third was a physician, Dr. Gustavus Adolphus Henry Darden). In 1895 he served in the legislature as floterial representative from Wilson and Smith counties. He was a charter member of Mt. Juliet Lodge No. 642, Free & Accepted Masons. He died on June 24, 1915, at the age of 80, and is buried in Fairmont Cemetery, Mt. Juliet.

The 1970s

The 10 years that began in 1970 have been crowded with events, great and small, like all other decades. It was the best of times, it was the worst of times. Not as expansive and optimistic as the preceding two decades, the 1970s did produce individual news events that were as significant as many others of the 150 years of history that Lebanon celebrated in a highly successful Sesquicentennial Celebration of its first municipal charter, held from September 27 to October 4, 1969.

The significance of the long impasse between the city government and the federal Environmental Protection Administration cannot yet be measured. While the city could quickly recover from the flurry of a police scandal or the morbid fascination with a sensational homicide, the effect of this crisis will be longer lasting and, informed persons believe, perhaps nothing less than disastrous. In 1971 Lebanon proposed to construct a waste treatment plant on Barton's Creek off Hartmann Drive. Government agencies said the plant must be built at the mouth of Barton's Creek. The city agreed. The EPA then reversed itself. By that time the city government realized that the river plant would cost far less but the federal agency insisted on the Hartmann Drive site. From that time on it was a head-butting situation. Meanwhile a moratorium on new sewer connections was imposed and

After retirement as county agricultural agent, James E. Ward turned his know-how into a successful ham processing business, selling hickory-smoked, naturally aged hams from a log smokehouse in his backyard to customers all over the country.

for all practical purposes annexation of any populated area to the City of Lebanon was blocked. Because the corporate area at that time provided almost no land for residential building, Lebanon's population growth was stalled at a critical point—under the 15,000 that many developers consider the minimum for new commercial and industrial locations. For that reason the choice of Lebanon by the Toshiba Company for a new electronics plant was greeted with relief and rejoicing. With strong urging by the administration of Gov. Ray Blanton, many of whose highly placed policy makers were from Wilson County, the Japanese company, one of the most progressive and dynamic in the industry, announced its decision in December 1977.

During the decade, meanwhile, West Wilson County had experienced great growth and in addition to hundreds of new homes and scores of new businesses the schools of that area kept pace with its progress. Because of this Mt. Juliet retained its identity as a viable community and was incorporated as a municipality with boundaries from Interstate 40 to U.S. 70. The eastern part of the county did not share in this growth, partly because of the difficulty of developing land there for subdivisions but principally because Nashville's ring growth had to that point been confined to a 25-mile radius in all directions. Because of the static population Watertown and its schools did not grow, and in 1979 the 16th Special School District was dissolved by referendum.

Changing population patterns are reflected in the new county commission, which supplanted the old county quarterly court after the adoption of a constitutional amendment by state voters in 1977. With only one commissioner from each voting district, the new 25-member body, whose presiding officer no longer has the title of county judge but is the county executive, has a majority of its members from west of U.S. 231. Because of the concentration of industrial and financial wealth in Lebanon, the county seat retains its identity as the center of county life but, like Hendersonville and Franklin, the city feels the strong tug of Metropolitan Nashville and by 1990 may be reduced to the role of satellite, much as Donelson in Davidson County was reduced in the 1950s.

However, the financial community of Lebanon has expanded tremendously since 1969. Besides the existing Commerce Union, Lebanon, and Peoples Banks, during the 1970s the First National Bank was established along with 10 additional locations for the older banks, other than their main offices. Besides First Federal Savings & Loan Association (established in 1929 as the State Building & Loan Association), Fidelity Federal and First State associations opened offices. Lebanon also is a center of health care for the area. The Wilson County Mental Health Center was established in 1972 with a staff of five. In 1971 a new wing was added to McFarland Hospital. In 1972 Extendicare, Inc., acquired the hospital. Accreditation was achieved, and in 1973 ownership was transferred to Humana, Inc. In 1977 construction was begun on the new University Medical Center in western Lebanon. The first phase was a one-level, 65-bed hospital that included departments of specialty care.

Always a center of education and once widely known as "The Little Athens of the South," Lebanon saw the development of all its school facilities during the decade. Cumberland College of Tennessee reached its highest enrollment in history early in the decade, although this growth slackened for a time. Castle Heights Military Academy went through a crisis when the Macfadden Foundation lessened its interest in the preparatory school. In 1974 the Castle Heights Foundation, composed chiefly of alumni and Lebanon residents, bought the school. Heights had be-

Built in 1923, this was the Lebanon High School building until it burned in March 1936. The high school, the junior high school, and Highland Heights elementary school were all housed in the large brick structure.

come coeducational in 1973 and began to emphasize enrollment of day students, not only from Wilson but from eastern Davidson County. Still a military school, the academy was in 1979 one of only 27 such schools in the United States. In 1973 Friendship Christian School opened its doors in the educational unit of the College Street Church of Christ; in five years it acquired its own buildings on Coles Ferry Pike and offered a full elementary and secondary school program.

In the arts, Lebanon and Wilson County moved more rapidly perhaps than in any other area. The Bicentennial year produced one lasting result, establishment of the Sound and Light theater company. Besides this dramatic company, music has attracted interest with organization of the Cumberland College Singers and the handbell choir, using the Richard Lawlor memorial bells, a television program originating in Lebanon, and the commissioning of a cello concerto for the Nashville Symphony Orchestra underwritten by Dr. and Mrs. Joe Bryant. The Pickin' Post recording studio is located in Lebanon; Bradley's Barn in western Wilson County was the first major recording facility associated with Music City. Artists with a national reputation came to live in Wilson County, beginning in the 1950s with Burl Ives and including Charley Daniels in Mt. Juliet, Curly Putman and Sonny Throckmorton on Franklin Road near Gladeville, Bill Anderson on Coles Ferry Pike, and, for half a year on Franklin Road while recording in Nashville, Paul McCartney and his wife Linda. In

October 1979 Putman, Throckmorton, and Anderson won citations at the annual Country Music Celebration.

In the field of letters books by Will Campbell of Mt. Juliet and the late Bowen (Mrs. Dan) Ingram of Lebanon received national attention, while Herschel Ligon, Green Hill farmer, figured in one of the books by Studs Terkel. Myles Horton of the Highlander School, whose formative years were spent in Lebanon, was the subject of a two-hour interview by Bill Moyers on national television.

Some Representative Men and Women

Samuel Barton

In 1846 the historian Albigence Waldo Putnam found the original Cumberland Compact in an old trunk which had belonged to Samuel Barton, one of the 256 men who had signed the document and one of the 12 representatives in the Tribunal of Notables, or General Arbitrators, who first governed the infant Cumberland settlements. Written in a fair hand and signed on May 13, 1780, the document lacked its first page and was mutilated and defaced on its second but it is still a remarkable tribute to the faith that Americans have in written law.

Barton was born in Virginia in January 1749 and was bound as an apprentice as a youth. In 1774 he took part in Lord Dunmore's War as a ranger and during the American Revolution served in the Seventh Virginia Regiment, Morgan's Rifles. Whether he came to Nashborough with James Robertson's party is not known but he told his son Gabriel that he had come "when there were but four families residing in the place." At any rate, Samuel Barton signed the compact, was shot in the wrist with an Indian rifle ball a few days before the Battle of the Bluff in April 1781, and served as one of the Notables. In 1783 a second compact was drawn up and signed by 10 leaders, including Barton; in April of that year, when North Carolina established the county of Davidson, he was appointed a justice of the peace. The county court then elected Barton entry taker. He became second major of militia, and a commissioner of the new town of Nashville. When Davidson County became a county of the new state of Tennessee in 1796 he was commissioned one of the justices of the peace and colonel of militia.

But in 1798, not yet 50 years of age, Samuel Barton gave up all of this and moved with his family to what would the next year become Wilson County, to a large plantation on Jennings' Fork of Round Lick Creek. He took up the vocation of surveyor in addition to his extensive farming operations, and appraised land and allocated lots in the new town of Lebanon.

Undoubtedly one of the reasons Barton left Nashville was the dispute over disposition of the funds of Davidson Academy and the matter of 640 acres of land given the Rev. Thomas Craighead to persuade him to come to Nashville as preacher and teacher at the Academy. On September 4, 1797, Samuel Barton filed a lawsuit against two members of the Academy board of trustees, Lardner Clarke and James Robertson. Craighead's daughter had married Robertson's son, and the family ties made the issue even more sensitive. Already the matter had cost Barton £640 hard money and threatened to cost him as sole solvent surety up to £900 which he sought to recover from the trustees. The dates of the suit and Barton's removal coincide, so it is reasonable to suppose some connection. In May 1810 Samuel Barton died.

William Bowen Campbell

A major base of the United States Army, located between Clarksville, Tennessee, and Hopkinsville, Kentucky, is named Fort Campbell. In the office of the commanding general hangs a picture of William Bowen Campbell. It is he for whom the fort was named. Born in Sumner County on February 1, 1807, he studied law with his uncle, Governor David Campbell of Virginia, and also studied with the noted St. George Tucker. He then began the practice of law in Smith County, Tennessee. In 1833 he became attorney-general of the district; in 1835 he was elected to the General Assembly. He resigned in 1836 to lead a company of Tennesseans to the Florida War.

Returning to Carthage, Campbell was elected as a Whig to

Congress for three terms, 1837 to 1843, and he became Colonel of the First Tennessee Regiment of Volunteers in 1846 when the Mexican War broke out. He fought with conspicuous gallantry at Monterrey, Matamoras, Vera Cruz, and Cerro Gordo. At Monterrey he coined the phrase that was to become famous: instead of ordering a charge, the commander cried, "Boys, follow me!" The war over, Campbell became judge of the fourth judicial circuit from 1847 to 1850. In 1851, after a memorable canvass against his old friend. General William Trousdale, Campbell was elected the last Whig governor of Tennessee. He declined re-election and accepted the presidency of the Bank of Middle Tennessee at Lebanon in 1853, moving to the former Seawell home on Coles Ferry Pike, which he renamed Camp Bell. In 1861 he campaigned vigorously for the preservation of the Union during two referenda. When offered command of all the forces to be raised in Tennessee for the Confederacy he declined but accepted a commission as a brigadier general in the United States Army, after assurance from President Lincoln that he need not take up arms against his native state. In August 1865 he was elected as a Conservative Unionist to the U.S. Congress. He died at Camp Bell during this term, on August 19, 1867.

Edward Everett Adams

Energetic, dynamic, and enterprising—a man of vision and faith in the future—Edward Everett Adams typifies the man of business in an expanding economy. He was born near Mt. Juliet in 1867, attended the country schools, enrolled in Cumberland University, and entered public life as a bookkeeper. In 1888 he leased a newspaper, *The Lebanon Herald,* and edited it for nine months in association with Dr. R. L. C. White before acquiring ownership with borrowed money, and changing the name to *The Lebanon Democrat.* In addition to this operation, he installed and operated the first telephone system in Lebanon while a bookkeeper for Anderson Drug Company; he operated the first motion picture house in Lebanon, the Nickel-O; and founded the Lyric Theatre. He owned the Lebanon Opera House, the Lebanon Garage, the Adams Outdoor Advertising Company, and a farm of 374 acres. In 1902 he installed the first Linotype machine used by a county newspaper in Middle Tennessee. He was active in the Knights of Pythias and the Odd Fellows, and was chief clerk of the State House of Representatives for three terms. He was secretary-treasurer of Cedarcroft Sanitarium, secretary of the Sunday School of the Lebanon Methodist Church and a member of the Board of Stewards, and was city clerk for many years. He died December 6, 1945.

Gemma Gause Adams

On May 25, 1893, Gemma Gause, daughter of Major S. S. Gause, editor of *The Springfield Herald*, and Portia Davis Gause, was married to Edward E. Adams. Born December 6, 1867, at Jacksonport, Arkansas, where her father had gone to practice law after the ending of the Civil War, she returned with her family to Tennessee two years later. She typified the active, public-spirited woman able to rear a family, direct a home, and enjoy a successful career of her own.

A founding member of the Tennessee Press & Authors Club, she was one of the first women editors in the state, and wrote articles published in various periodicals in the South. She collected one of the most extensive private libraries in the state. She was active in the work of the Daughters of the American Revolution, the United Daughters of the Confederacy, the Parent-Teacher Association, and the Methodist Church, and was a charter member of the American Legion Auxiliary, Post 15. She served as member and chairman of the State Democratic executive committee. She was literary and society editor of *The Lebanon Democrat* and when other business activity occuped her husband she managed its editorial affairs. She was the mother of a son, Alfred A. Adams, IV, and a daughter, Sydney Virginia Adams Thackston. On September 24, 1931, at the age of 63 she died at her home on West Main Street.

Sara Hardison

She often said she was on a first name basis with more practicing lawyers in America than any other person. They all called her "Miss Sara." She was law librarian of Cumberland University for 40 years and taught legal bibliography on an individual basis to over 4000 law students.

Sara Hardison came to Lebanon as a child when her father opened the first cash grocery in Lebanon in 1914. She attended Cumberland University and received the Bachelor of Laws degree in 1923, becoming the law librarian in the same year. Cumberland had accepted women law students at an early date, and there were enough in the 1920s to justify the establishment of a chapter of Iota Tau Tau legal fraternity for women in 1929 through the efforts of Miss Hardison, who became a national officer.

The Cordell Hull law library was her domain and students said, "If Miss Sara can't find the law or the case on any subject it probably does not exist." Gov. Leroy Collins of Florida, on his way to chair the National Democratic Convention in 1956, made a special stop in Nashville to drive out to see "Miss Sara." She was for many years a Kentucky Colonel, on the staff of the Governor of Kentucky, through the favor of a former law student.

Retiring in 1961 when the law school was removed to Birmingham, she died June 3, 1979, Her pallbearers included nine former Cumberland students, the president of the college, the dean, and the chairman of the alumni association.

Ethel Rawnsley Thompson

On November 19, 1963, Ethel Rawnsley Thompson was buried in Hearn Hill Cemetery near Watertown, according to the rites of the Episcopal Church. She had been born in Bingley, Yorkshire, England, on March 11, 1886, and christened in the Church of England.

In 1913 she had emigrated to the United States by way of Canada. During the first World War she was employed in Washington, D.C., with the Federal Railroad Administration and there met William M. Thompson of Watertown, who became her husband.

Mrs. Thompson and her mother, Mrs. S. A. Rawnsley, had come to Columbus, Ohio, to join the Rawnsley sons but a sister remained in England. After becoming a naturalized citizen of the United Staes in 1920, Mrs. Thompson returned to visit her sister, Mrs. Beatrice Brown of Maidstone, Kent, in 1921 and 1925 and again after the war of 1939–1945. These were brief visits; she had chosen Watertown as her home and resided in Wilson County for more than 30 years. Despite her long absence from her native country she retained a touch of Yorkshire in her speech as long as she lived: as the poet Rupert Brooke said, "There is some corner of a foreign field that is forever England."

For many years Mrs. Thompson was the Watertown correspondent for *The Lebanon Democrat.* She became known to all young men of the county when, after her husband's death, she was made secretary of the Wilson County Local Board 16 of the Selective Service System and served in that office for the duration of the wartime draft, maintaining induction and service records and mailing the familiar "Greetings from the President" over the signature of Walter D. Ferrell, chief clerk.

Cordelia McElrath Norris Gwynn

For 40 years Cordelia Gwynn served as a teacher and visiting Jeanes supervisor, a position funded by the Rosenwald Fund for Improvement of the Negro Race. She never ceased to search for new techniques and procedures for the public schools. Her interest in black history was unflagging and she contributed materially to the first published history of the black people of Wilson County.

She was born to Henry and Mary Irving McElrath in Watauga County, North Carolina, on January 7, 1905. She received a Bachelor of Science degree from Tennesssee A. & I. State University in 1928 and then began the work that brought her in contact with 22 black schools throughout Wilson County. In 1952 she received the Master of Science degree in supervision and administration. She sponsored and attended many education workshops, in reading, language, art, mathematics, and history. Mrs. Gwynn served under the administration of seven county superintendents of public instruction: W. H. Waters Sr., James E. Belcher, Carl Chaney, Ray Phillips, Ernest Cotten, Albert Jewell, and Erwin Reed. She died at Lincoln Hospital, the Bronx, New York, on May 24, 1970.

John Edgerton

One of the most influential industrialists of the 1920s was John Edgerton. He was president of the National Association of Manufacturers for 21 years and in 1924 was mentioned as a possible candidate for president of the United States.

He was born in Johnston County, North Carolina, in 1879, attended the common schools there, and came to Lebanon in 1892 with his brother, Dr. Howard K. Edgerton. He first attended Cumberland University, then received a Cartmell Scholarship to Vanderbilt where he took his Bachelor of Arts degree in 1902 and a Master's degree the following year. Becoming a teacher, first at Castle Heights School in Lebanon and then at Memphis University School, he founded Columbia Military Academy in 1905 and remained there for seven years.

In 1912 Dr. Edgerton, who had founded the Lebanon Woolen Mills three years earlier, asked his brother to join the company as secretary-treasurer and general manager. When Dr. Edgerton died in 1914, John Edgerton became president and guided the industry through the difficult years of the first World War and the Depression of the 1930s. He was founder of the Southern States Industrial Council, and became widely known as a speaker at industrial conferences throughout the United States. He was a Methodist, a member of Kappa Sigma fraternity, a Mason, and a conservative Democrat. Upon his death in 1938 he was succeeded in the presidency of the woolen mills by his nephew, Howard K. Edgerton, Jr.

Walter Jackson Baird

He collected his own insurance policy, took an airplane ride on his 100th birthday, was the oldest living active Rotarian, and probably helped more young married couples own their own homes than any other person who ever lived in Wilson County. Born near Baird's Mill on July 3, 1873, he grew up with ambitions to be a railway mail clerk and took his first job in the I. B.

The production line at the Lebanon Woolen Mills was Wilson County's leading industry for 50 years after its founding in 1908. During World War II the company received the "E" Award from the US Marine Corps for efficiency in production.

Castleman general store at Gladeville because the post office was located there. Gladeville then contained about 100 inhabitants, three stores, two blacksmith shops, two churches, a woodworking shop, Woodrum's saddlery, and a high school. While he worked he studied for the civil service examination and he passed. Openings for railway mail clerks were scarce and he went home to wait. Meanwhile Robert Fakes heard about this ambitious young man and offered to sell him his store at Holloway. Young Baird bought it and, because it contained the post office, became a postmaster. He also established a produce wagon route to Nashville. In 1903 Rural Free Delivery was established and the post office was closed. The main attraction having been removed, he sold the store and thought about moving West. Instead he moved to Lebanon and took a job as bookkeeper for McClain Brothers, then went into partnership with Porter McClain as Cash Dry Goods Company.

In 1914 Frank Stratton asked Walter Baird to become cashier of the Union Bank & Trust Company. He remained until its merger with the Commerce Union system in 1923, then became a merchant again, buying the hardware store owned by H. W. Cook, whose building had burned in November 1923. Meanwhile, the State Building & Loan Association had been formed in 1929 and Baird became its office manager in 1934. He became president and, upon retirement from active business, chairman of the board until his death. He also was a partner in Tennessee Hereford Farms; member of the 10th district school board; trustee of Cumberland University; donor with his wife, Ethel Bouton Baird, of the restored chapel at Memorial Hall which was then named Baird Chapel. An elder of the Presbyterian Church and choir member, he attended several of the Billy Graham Crusades after he became 90 years old. On his 100th birthday in 1973 he was honored by receiving a letter from President Nixon, recognition from Governor Dunn, and a proclamation by Mayor Willis H. Maddox. The new junior high school was named Walter J. Baird Junior High School. He died February 16, 1980, in his 107th year.

Robert S. Burton

On October 9, 1911, in the LaGuardo community, Robert S. Burton was born. He attended the public schools and received a Bachelor of Laws degree from Cumberland University in 1933. In 1936 he was elected a member of the Wilson County quarterly court.

When the second World War came Burton enlisted in the U.S. Marine Corps and served in the Pacific Theater of Operations with the 4th Marine Division. Returning to civilian life in 1945 he was a successful candidate for the state House of Representatives the following year. He operated the family farm and continued as a member of the county court and commission, representing the 4th district, until his death. He also served as a member of the Wilson County American Revolution Bicentennial Commission. He was a member of the LaGuardo Church of Christ.

In 1969 during the Lebanon Sesquicentennial celebration Burton was a tall, impressive Uncle Sam, wearing the traditional suit of stars and stripes.

He died October 21, 1979. His son, Robert Samuel Burton, Jr., succeeded to the seat on the county commission. County Executive Don Simpson eulogized Burton as "a great magistrate and commissioner who served the community with long, faithful service."

DALLAS YOUNG
Fire Chief, City of Lebanon,
1917–1962.

CHARLES LOYD
Mayor of Lebanon, 1961–1971

W. LEE HARRIS
First principal, four-year
Lebanon High School,
established 1918

ALICE MORGAN DOAK
Dean of Nurses, McFarland
Hospital, 1942–1957.
R.N., 1909

NATHAN GREEN, JR.
Law Teacher, Chancellor,
Cumberland University,
1856–1919

HARRY PHILLIPS
Senior Judge, U.S. Sixth Circuit
Court of Appeals

Suggested Readings

Albright, Edward. *Early History of Middle Tennessee.* Nashville, 1909.

Bone, Winstead Paine. *A History of Cumberland University.* Lebanon, 1935.

Caldwell, Joshua W. *Bench and Bar of Tennessee.* Knoxville: Ogden Brothers, 1898.

Carr, John. *Early Times in Middle Tennessee.* Nashville, 1857. (Reprint edition by Horsley & Associates, 1958.)

Davis, Giles. *The Life and Times of Rev. Andrew Davis.* Lebanon, 1907.

Drake, James Vaulx. *An Historical Sketch of Wilson County, Tennessee.* Nashville, 1879. (Reprint edition by Wilson County American Revolution Bicentennial Commission, 1976.)

————. *The Life of Genl. Robert Hatton.* Nashville, 1867.

Gray, John W. *The Life of Joseph Bishop.* Nashville, 1858. (Reprint edition by The Reprint Company, Spartanburg, S.C., 1974.)

Grime, John Harvey. *The History of Middle Tennessee Baptists.* Nashville: Baptist & Reflector, 1902. (Reprint edition by Hall Grime, 1972.)

Goodspeed Publishing Company. *History of Tennessee, From the Earliest Time To the Present.* Chicago, 1886-1887. (Reprint edition of volume with county sketches of Maury, Williamson, Rutherford, Wilson, Bedford, and Marshall by Woodward & Stinson, Columbia, TN 1971.)

Green, Nathan. *Echoes From Caruthers Hall.* Nashville: Cumberland Presbyterian Publishing House, 1889.

Hale, Will T., and Dixon L. Merritt. *A History of Tennessee and Tennesseans.* 8 vols., Chicago and New York: Lewis, 1913.

History Associates. *The History of Wilson County: Its Land and Its Life.* Lebanon: Wilson County, 1961.

Holland, Cecil F. *Morgan and His Raiders.* New York, 1942.

Killebrew, J. B. *Introduction to the Resources of Tennessee.* Nashville, 1874. (Reprint edition by The Reprint Company, Spartanburg, S.C., 1974.)

Macon, Drake, Alice Chastain, Herschel Ligon. *The History of Green Hill.* Lebanon: Democrat, 1946.

Phillips, Harry. *Phillips Family History.* Lebanon: Democrat, 1935.

Sloan, Gene H. *With Second Army Somewhere in Tennessee.* Murfreesboro, 1956.

Walker, Hugh Frazier. *Tennessee Tales.* Nashville: Aurora, 1970.

Wallace, Louis D. *Makers of Millions.* Nashville: Tennessee Department of Agriculture, 1951.

Index

Illustrations are indicated by an asterisk following the page number.

Adams, Edward Everett, 115–116
Adams, Gemma Gause, 116
Agriculture, vii, x, 77, 105
Alcorn, Elijah, 24–25
Alcorn, John, 17, 21, 25, 33
Alexander, Benjamin, 8
Alexander, George, 9
Allen, Eliza, 25–26
Allen, John, 25–26
Allen, William, 14, 19, 22
Anderson, James, 19, 22
Asbury, Bishop Francis, 52–53
Atkinson, Joe, 104–105

Bailey, Joseph D., 98
Baird, Walter Jackson, 119–121
Baird, William Donnell, xiii, 102–105, 104*
Bairds Mill, 43, 44
Banks and banking, 67, 76, 78, 106–107, 111
Barnett, Robert E., 95
Barr, S.B.F.C., 60–61
Barry, James L., 45
Barton, Samuel, 12, 113–114
Baxter, Jere, xii
Beard, Leonard, 95
Beard, Richard, 51
Belcher, William Andrew, 95
Bell, John 29
Blacks, 58–62
Bond, Elder John, 54
Bowers, J.F. & Bros., 19
Bratten, Clyde O., 70
Bringhurst, Edward, 69
Brown, Ernest L., 95, 97
Bryant, James, 61
Buchanan, Frank, 74, 75
Burke, Efford, 85-86
Burkett, Robert, 68-69
Burton, Robert S., 121–122

Cain, George, viii
Cainsville, viii
Calhoun, Thomas, 51
Campbell, William Bowen, x, xii, 31, 33, 101, 114–115
Cannon, Newton, 28-30
Carmack, Edward Ward, 65–66
Carr, Marvin, 61
Carter, W.W., x
Cartmell, William, 97
Caruthers, Robert Looney, x, xi, 25, 30*, 31–32, 33, 36–37
Castle Heights Military Academy, xii, 74, 76, 91*, 111–112
Cedars of Lebanon State Park, 78, 86–90
Center Hill, 8–9
Chambers, William Richard, 36
Chenault, Joseph J., 95
Church of Christ, 54
Civil War, 40–50
Clement, Frank Goad, 32*
Clover Bottom, store at, 21–22
Cloyd, John, 8
Coble, Bert, 40
Commerce, viii, xii–xiii, 21, 22, 62, 63
Confederate officers, 41
Conyer, Thomas: water mill of, 12
Cook, Valentine, 52
Cooper, Christopher, 18
Cotton, William M., 72
Country life, 55–58
Courthouses, xi, 19–20
Court of pleas and quarter sessions, 17, 21*
Coy, Ben, 90
Craig, John H., 68
Crawford, Tom, 94
Crutcher, Edward, 22
Cumberland Presbytery, 33–34, 51
Cumberland School of Law, 35–36, 37, 40, 101

Cumberland University, x, xi, 33–40, 34*, 39*, 45, 48, 67, 70, 74, 78, 93, 100, 105, 111, 117

Daniel, Robert E., 73
Davis, Andrew, 59
Davis, Newburn, 56
D-Day, 94–95
Deeds, earliest, 12
Democrats, 29
Dixon Lanier Merritt Nature Center, 89
Doak, John, 17, 18
Donnell, George V., 76
Donnell, Robert, 33, 51
Donnell, Samuel, 50–51
Drake, Brittain, 25
Drake's Lick, 8, 11
Dressler, James, 40
DuBois, W.E.B., 59

Early explorers, 2
Ebenezer Campground, 52
Edgerton, John, xiii, 119
Elam, Elder E.A., 54
Electricity, 64–65, 67
Entertainers, 85, 86
EPA controversy, 109–110
Eskew, Herman, 95
Establishment of county, 3, 15–20
Evertson, Annie, 26

Faulkner, Walter S., 74–75*
Ferrell, Gladys, 87, 88
Fessler, John Richard, 98–99
Figures, Matthew, 17, 18
Finley, Jesse, 28, 29, 100–101
Finley, Obadiah G., 28
Firestone, 103–104
Fisk Jubilee Singers, 59
Fite, John A., 41, 46, 47, 59
Forrest, Nathan Bedford, 43, 91
Forrester, Eugene, 99–100
Foster, John, 8, 11
Foster, Robert Verrell, 51–52
Freeman, Thomas Harvey, 108–109
Friendship Christian School, 112
Fugate, Terence, 81

Gerhardt, Charles Hunter, 94–95
Gettysburg, 41–42, 45–48
Gilreath, Samuel Burham, 36
Gladeville, 105, 120
Godson, W.F., 74, 76

Golladay, Edward I., xi, 33
Golladay, Frederick, 26
Golladay, Isaac, 26, 27
Gore, Albert, 27, 32
"Grand Ole Opry," 82–86
Grannis, William, x
Green, Grafton, 35–36, 37
Green, Nathan, 35, 36, 37*, 125*
Green Hill, 11, 44, 105–106
Grime, John Harvey, 54
Grisham, William, x
Gulf Red Cedar Co., 67
Guthrie, Chloe Babb, 52
Gwynn, Cordelia McElrath Norris, 118–119

Hancock, Nelson D., 14–15
Hancock, Walter, 65
Hardison, Sara, 116–117
Harkreader, Fiddlin' Sid (Sidney Johnson), 82–83*, 85
Harper, Ellis, 66
Harpole, John, 7, 17,18
Harpole petition, 16, 18
Hatcher, J.J., 64, 65
Hatcher, John, 77
Hatton, Robert Hopkins, 33, 41, 43*, 46, 50, 100
Hay, George, 84
Haynes, B.F., 53
Haynes, Paul, 97
Hays, Harry Thompson, 100
Head, William Kenneth, 61
Hickory Ridge, 11
Hightower, Billy M., 102
Hobbs, Avis T., 68, 97
Holloway, Thomas Jefferson, 41
Houston, Sam, 21, 25–27, 28, 31
Howard, John K., 41
Hunt, R.E. & Co., 20
Hutchings, John, 22

Impson, John & Thomas, 14, 22
Indians, 6–7, 10–11
Industry, vii, x, xii, 8, 63, 65, 67, 76–77, 101–105, 110
Ingram, Bowen, 80, 113

Jackson, Andrew, 20–22, 27, 28, 29
Jackson, Jack, 84–85
Jacobs, Edward, 12–15, 22
Jacobs, Layula, 12, 13, 15
Jelley, Michael E., 87, 88

Jennings, Elby, 63
Johnson, Perry, 27
Jones, Eva Thompson, 84
Jones, James Chamberlain, viii, 30–31

Kelley, David Campbell, 48–49
Kelley, Lavinia, 53
Kirkpatrick, John Dillard, 48
Knowles, James E., 95
Korean War, 97

Lancaster, Jerry David, 98
Lancaster, John, 12, 18
Lancaster, Tom, 59
Land grants and recipients, 9–10
Lebanon, 14, 18–19, 22, 25, 28, 43, 44,
   45, 53, 64–68, 92, 100, 101–105, 109–
   112; city administration, 74–75, 77–78;
   establishment, 18–19; first settlers, 14,
   19; industrial subdivision, 102, 103;
   public square, ix; sesquicentennial
   celebration, xiv, 109
Lebanon College for Young Ladies, xii
Lebanon Flour Milling Co., x
Lebanon High School, 112*
Lebanon Theological Seminary, 38, 51
Lebanon Woolen Mills, xii, 66*, 67, 77,
   78, 119, 120*
Lee, Robert E., 42, 47–48

McClain, Josiah, 11, 76
McClain, William, 8, 11, 17, 21
McDaniel, Frank, 76
Macon, Uncle Dave, 82
McElroy, Maude Woodfork, (Aunt
   Jemima), 59
Macfadden, Bernarr, 74
MacPherson, Cornelius Gregory, 23,
   33, 34
Maddux, John B., 95
Mail delivery, 67
Manier, W.M., 59–60, 61
Martin, Andrew Bennett, 36
Martin, George W., 107*
Martin, John, 32
Mason, Laura, 76
Merritt, Dixon, xii, 11, 65, 80, 86, 89
Merritt petition, 15, 18
Methodist Church, 52–53
Militia officers, first, 17
Minty, R.H.G., 44–45
Mitchell, David Earle, xii
Mitchell, Edward, 14, 17, 18, 19, 22

Mizell, Virginia Prewett, 81
Moore, Mrs. B.D., 55–56, 56–58
Moore, William, 53
Morgan, John Hunt, 43–45, 48, 90–91
Mt. Juliet, 106–109, 108*, 110
Murrell, John, 90

Neal, Ross, 69
Neil, Albert Bramlett, 36
Norris, A.D., 47
Norene Telephone Exchange, 57*

Organ, John Chartres, 23
"Our Folks," 80

Parrish, W. Collier, 87–88
Patterson, Malcolm, 65–66
Patton, George S., 91–92
Pendleton, Lewis, 69
Pentecostalism, 53
Phillips, James Madison, 49
Phillips, John & Benjamin, 8
Pick-up, 56–58
Polk, James Knox, 28–31
Presbyterian Church, USA, 34, 38
Price, Horace, 61
Price, M.A., ix–x, 61
Progressive Era, 62–68

Radio, 81–86
Railroads, x–xi, xii, 63, 66–67, 106
Red cedar, 86–87, 88
Religion, 50–55
Revival movement, 50, 52, 53
Rice, Cale Young, 81
Rice, Laban Lacy, 76, 81
Richardson, Edwin W., 97
Roads, ix, xiii, 62, 76, 106
Roane, John Selden, 100
Robertson, John Fite, 68, 70
Rogers, Jeff, 6–7
Rose, Walter, 79–80
Ross Gear & Tool Co., 101, 103
Rousseau, Lovell, 90

Sacred Harp singing, 53
Saloons, xii
Scofield, Cyrus Ingerson, 54–55
Scott, Miller W., 97
Sealey, Bill, 59
Settlers, first, 7–12
7th Tennessee infantry regiment, 41–42,
   46, 47, 48

Shannon, Harry B., 71–72
Shannon, Homer, 71–73
Shannon's Drug Store, 70–73
Shepard, Sam G., 47, 49–50
Simmons, Mintus and family, 61
Sloan, Ralph, 85
Smith, George Washington, 12
Smotherman, Donald, 95
Sorrells, Hardie, 73
Spring Creek Presbysterian Church, 8, 50
Stanley, Robert, Jr., 97
Statesville, 8
Steele, William, 17, 18
Stewart, Alexander P., 100
Stiles, E.D., drug store, 71
Smith, Bill, 66

Tax list of 1795, 11
Taylor, Margaret Nelson, 12
Taylor, Perrigan & Sarah Nelson, 11–12
Teachers, 36, 56
Tennessee Maneuver Area, 92–93
Tennessee Mfg. Co., x
The Lebanon Banner, 74–75, 77
The Lebanon Democrat, xii, 67, 90, 97–98, 99, 115, 116, 118
Thompson, Joseph, 70
Thompson, David Upham, 70
Thompson, Ethel Rawnsley, 117–118
Thompson, Uncle Jimmy (James Donald), 82, 83–84
Town Spring, 14, 18, 67–68
Transportation, 79*. See also Railroads, Roads.
Trigg, Alanson, 18
Tucker, George, 72
Turney, Henry, 12
'Twenties, the, 70–78
29th Infantry Division, 94

Unionists, 63
United Daughters of Confederacy, 46*

Vietnam War, 97–99; casualties, 98

Walker, Edward Glenn, 78–80

Walker, John B., 7
Wallace, Carl, 99
Walls, Claude, 97
Ward, James E., 110*
Waste disposal systems, xiv, 109–110
Waters, Edgar, 77
Waters, Wilson Lawrence, 62–63
Watertown, 45, 62–64*, 103, 110
Wauford, J.R., 63
Webster, Willie, 95
Wharton, Jesse, 32
Wheeler, Joseph, 44, 45, 91
Whigs, 29
Whited, Lee, 69
Williams, J.T., 56
Williamson, Charles, 77
Williamson, Elizabeth, 8
Williamson, John & Margaret Cloyd, 8, 21
Wilson County: arts in, 112–113; boundaries, 3, 15, 16–17, 18; churches, 106, 107; civil districts, 17–18, 20; climate, 5–6; commission, 20, 110–111; congressmen, 33; geology of, 5; health care, 111; immigration into, 22–25; integration, 60–61; judge, 79; Justices of Peace, first, 17; location, 1; map, 4; out-migration, viii, 105; population, vii, viii, 58,107; rivers and creeks, 3; silk manufacturing in, viii; suburban growth, xiv, 105–109; surface water, 3–5; village formation in, vii
Wilson County Fair, viii
Wilson County Holiness Camp Ground, 53
Winston, George Wharton, 59
Winter, Dr. W.J., 63
Woodall, Andrew Oscar, 95
Wooten, Paul, 80–81
World War I, 68–70; casualties, 69
World War II, 90–96; casualties, 96
Wynne, Albert, 28
Wynne, John, 8, 12, 17, 18, 20

Young, David, 8
Young, James, 8, 11

G. Frank Burns was born at Milan, Tennessee, in 1921. After taking a law degree at Cumberland he became a reporter and editor with *The Lebanon Democrat.* He was also a correspondent for the *Nashville Banner, The Tennessean,* UPI, and *The Christian Science Monitor,* publishing articles in *Time* and *Newsweek* as well.

In 1967, after taking an MA at George Peabody College, he became Public Relations Director and Chairman of Publications at Cumberland College. Under his direction the student newspaper won an All-American rating. In 1973 he earned a doctorate in English at Vanderbilt University.

Dr. Burns has studied at Oxford University, the University of London, and the Shakespeare Centre of the University of Birmingham at Stratford-on-Avon. He has also done research at Princeton and the Huntington Library. He is working on a biography of Joe L. Evins and a study of Allen Tate. Since 1974 he has been a member of the English Department at Tennessee Technological University at Cookeville.

He was coordinating editor of the *History of Wilson County,* published in 1961 under the auspices of the Tennessee Historical Commission. In 1976, as Heritage Area Chairman of the County American Revolution Bicentennial Commission, he edited a series of historical newsletters and wrote the introductory essay for a reprint edition of Drake's *Historical Sketch of Wilson County, Tennessee.* In January 1977 he became county historian. He also edits *The Historian,* a quarterly newsletter of History Associates of Wilson County.